D0842959

ROUGHSTOCK

the mud, the blood, and the beer

TY MURRAY
Kendra Santos

ROUGHSTOCK

the mud, the blood, and the beer

TY MURRAY

Kendra Santos

EquiMedia

Austin, Texas

EQUIMEDIA

President   Kanjiro Tokita
Creative Director   Rachman Feinberg

ROUGHSTOCK
the mud, the blood, and the beer

Authors   Ty Murray
            Kendra Santos
Assistant Editor   Carolyn S. Pryor
Graphic Designers   Victoria J. Allen
                      Rachman Feinberg
Photographers   Armindo Almeida
                  Jeff Belden
                  Cowpix
                  John Crowther
                  Jim Fain
                  Jerry Gustafson
                  Dan Hubbell
                  David Jennings
                  Gary Jensen
                  Tim Mantoani
                  Fred Nyulassy
                  Jori Peck
                  Mark Reis
                  Richard Roschke
                  Sue Rosoff
                  Kendra Santos
                  Louise Serpa
                  Jennifer Silverberg
                  Jan Spencer
                  Shari Van Alsburg
                  Andy Watson

Library of Congress Cataloging-in-Publication Data

Murray, Ty, 1969-
    Roughstock: the mud, the blood, and the beer / Ty Murray,
Kendra Santos.
        p. cm.
    Includes index.
    ISBN 0-9625898-7-X
    1. Murray, Ty, 1969- 2. Rodeo performers--United States--
Biography. 3. Bull riding--United States. I. Santos, Kendra, 1961-
II. Title.

    GV1833.6.M88 A3 2000
    791.8'4--dc21
    [B]   2001018801

Published by
EquiMedia Corporation
P.O. Box 90519
Austin, TX 78709
Tel: 512-821-0609
Fax: 512-821-0608

Printed in China by Prosperous Printing Co., Ltd.
10 9 8 7 6 5 4 3
06 05 04 03 02

I want to thank my mom and dad, Butch and Joy, and sisters, Kim and Kerri, for your love and friendship throughout my life. You've all supported everything I've ever done with interest and pride, and I appreciate that more than you know. Mom and Dad, I realize how hard you worked to support what you knew I loved to do, even back in the days when my rodeoing was an expensive habit with no chance of any financial return. Thanks, Dad, for running alongside those calves with a finger stuck in my beltloop, and Mom, for cheating on those alligators so I could make the whistle.

I want to thank Cody Lambert and Jim Sharp for all the things I talk about in this book. There's nothing here that we haven't talked about and done a thousand times. Thanks, Klete and Razor, for all your help and for being great examples to learn from. You guys are my buddies.

I want to thank Kendra Santos for years of friendship and hundreds of hours spent learning about my life, and how and why I do things so we could put it on paper. We worked around the clock, in the van on the way home from rodeos and holed up in hotel rooms between rodeo and PBR performances. Thanks for being a sport, like the time I put my bull rope around my couch and pushed you off the side to help you understand how bull riders use their free arms for balance.

Thanks to all my family, friends, fans and sponsors — Wrangler, CLS Transportation Service, Resistol, Dan Post Boots, Las Vegas, and Sierra Sports — for sticking by me through thick and thin. When I was half bucked off it was you — screaming your lungs out — who helped me get to the whistle. Thanks for believing in me, and for being there to share this ride.

CONTENTS

(PRCA Photo by Mark Reis)

Legends. (Kendra Santos photo)

Preface

by Larry Mahan

I remember watching a young 13-year-old rodeo cowboy warming up for the bull riding event at the National Little Britches Rodeo Association Finals in Colorado Springs. His physical exercises were that of a gymnast before a meet. Mentally, I could see that he had total concentration and dedication to his sport of rodeo. Barring injury, this young man was going to be one of rodeo's greatest champions. He rode a tough bull that night...one that could possibly have slipped out from under me in my glory days.

I invited that young man to spend some time at the Saddle Soar Ranch that summer. I knew I should have knocked him in the head then...it was obvious that Ty Murray was going to rewrite rodeo's record books.

By the time Ty had won his seventh world all-around championship, I was ecstatic. For the past 25 years I had to walk around looking in mirrors saying, "I'm the greatest," a line Muhammad Ali once used. Poor Ty Murray will have to do that forever. I predict that no one will ever win eight world champion all-around cowboy belt buckles, especially in the three most physically, mentally and emotionally demanding events in rodeo, the bareback riding, saddle bronc riding and bull riding.

Great job, Ty Murray...You are the greatest.

Larry Mahan
Camp Verde, Texas
Six-time World Champion All-Around Cowboy,
1965 and '67 World Champion Bull Rider

Introduction
In Pursuit of The Dream

Watching the rodeo with Bruce Ford. (Sue Rosoff photo)

When I was in fifth grade, my teacher, Mrs. Simmons, handed out a questionnaire one day that asked, "If you could do anything in your life, what would it be?" Without hesitating, I wrote, "I want to beat Larry Mahan's record," referring to his record six world all-around championships. My mom held onto that paper all these years and it's fun to look at now, but I've never needed it as a reminder because I've never stopped thinking about it. Everything I've done every day since — every workout, every practice session, every 3,000-mile drive, every wreck, every surgery, every thought — has been with that goal in mind.

None of what I've won has come easily. I've worked my butt off. When you rodeo for a living, there are no gimmies. Cowboys don't have coaches or personal trainers to stay after us and tell us what to do. We either want to win more than anything else on earth or we go home. Every day I was in that gym straining and sweating I'd get to thinking about the seventh all-around championship and what it might feel like to win it. Then I'd step my workout up another notch.

The thing I've concentrated on most my whole life is bearing down, gritting my teeth and trying my heart out every day, every ride. Because when it's all said and done, the guy who tries hardest wins. No one has ever wanted a seventh all-around championship more than me. That's why I got it. It sounds so simple, but that's how I see it. The bottom of your guts — that's where "try" comes from — is where world championships are won or lost.

When I won my first world all-around championship in 1989, a lot of people asked me if I was surprised by how well I was doing at such a young age and so early in my career. I reminded them that I didn't just wake up one day with a gold buckle on my belt. There was nothing sudden about it. World championships don't just sneak up on you. I was only 20, but I'd been working hard at that first championship for 18 years. It was a dream fulfilled, but I'd been climbing stepping stones to it since I was 2 years old.

One of the lessons I learned that first championship year was that there's a big difference between riding great and doing it every day. Learning how to maintain your peak performance level is a real challenge and a big test. It's a real trick to put aside the small details, like being tired or sick or not drawing at the top of the herd, and still ride at the top of your game day in and day out. So much goes into every championship. I don't care how much you win one by, or how many you win, a world championship means you were the very best in the game that year.

It makes me sick when people say, "He only won one world championship" about anyone, because you can't luck out and win one. That's impossible. A world championship is never a fluke. You can't draw perfect all year just like you can't draw bad all year. That's just an excuse that the law of averages takes care of over the course of a season. I also learned early on that you can't ever let up if you want to stay on top. If someone wants a championship worse than I do he'll win it.

Anything worth having in life is hard to get, and things that are easy to get or achieve generally don't mean much. I cherish the ranch I bought with rodeo earnings because it's taken everything I've had since I was 2 years old to get it. I have 1,861 acres of beautiful country, full of wildlife, with two lakes on it, and I appreciate it every day because I worked so hard for it. I didn't say, "I'd love to have a ranch, I wish I'd win the lottery." I didn't wait for money to fall out of the sky. I worked hard to be the very best I could be, and I saved every penny I could. I didn't set out to be the best cowboy in the world to get rich. If money's what I cared about I would have been a brain surgeon or a lawyer. I can't rodeo for free now because I'd starve to death. But for 18 years of my life I basically did it for nothing but the love of it. I wasn't making any money, but every little victory along the way paid off as a valuable stepping stone.

Rodeo taught me a good work ethic because nothing's handed to anyone. It's hard work, and the minute I stop putting 100 percent of my effort and attention into my riding will be the minute I'll stop expecting to win. I've also learned that to be a leader in any industry you have to work hard every day and keep striving for more or you'll get left in the dust. You can never be too good at what you do, and what you won yesterday doesn't mean squat today because bulls can't read your buckle. They don't know if I'm Ty Murray or Joe Blow, and they don't care. That adds dimension to this sport. When a boxer goes up against Mike Tyson, he watches the tapes. He studies his track record and bases his strategy on it. I have no way of knowing what a bull might do on any given day, and he doesn't get any previews of my riding style, either. I have to compete against him in that he's my obstacle, but I have to compete with him to win.

Rodeo is so humbling in so many ways, and I think that has a lot to do with why I'm still the same person now that I was when I started. I haven't forgotten that I'm the same guy who ate all that dirt when I was learning to ride calves. I still bite the dust when I don't bear down and do everything right. I still have cowboy values and the same outlook on life, and my handshake is still worth something. I had so many dreams when I was a kid, and feel so lucky for all of them that have come true. Don't get me wrong. I didn't luck out and win anything. But when you start working toward a bull riding championship when you're 2, with a whatever-it-takes attitude, it means more than I can say to win one (1993). Winning a second bull riding championship in 1998 was a dream come true all over again. Still, I can't imagine a greater feeling of self-satisfaction for me than winning the seventh world all-around championship.

MY LIFE

I'm a fourth-generation cowboy. My dad's maternal grandfather, Walter Schultz, and his six brothers, Guy, Clarence, Troy, Will, Grover and Floyd, worked on the famous 101 Ranch just south of Ponca City, Okla. The 101, which was owned by the Miller brothers, was so big that it had its own bank, store and sheriff. At that time, the 101 was the largest diversified ranch in the United States. The 101 was a working cattle ranch, but every exotic animal you can imagine — ostriches, camels, sea turtles, buffalo, you name it — lived there, too. The 101 also had a world-famous Wild West Show, and the Schultz brothers all rode in it.

There were no bucking chutes in the bronc riding back then, so muggers grabbed ahold of the broncs while the cowboys got up on them. Walter was a renowned mugger. He married a 14-year-old Potawatami Indian woman by the name of Josephine Papan. They lived on the 101 Ranch, in a tent on the Salt Fork River. The stories handed down to me claim she'd set trot lines (strings with hooks and bait hanging from them) across the river and catch 125-pound catfish. Then she hung them up and butchered them in a tree, just like you would a deer. That river was their life. They ate and drank from it, and even bathed in it. Walter and Josephine had a daughter named Georgia, who is my grandmother. She married my grandpa, Harold Murray, and they had a little boy they named Butch — my dad.

Walter's brother, my dad's Great Uncle Guy, rode broncs and bull-dogged buffalo in the 101 Ranch's Wild West Show. He jumped the buffalo from the running board of a car. Guy once rode the Hall of Fame bronc Midnight. He and another Schultz brother, Floyd, were the best wild horse racers and relay racers at a time when those events were big.

< At a high school rodeo after my hand came out of the riggin'. I landed on my feet thanks to gymnastics. (Gustafson photo)

Guy wrangled on the 101 with Bill Pickett, the famous black cowboy who invented bulldogging (also known as steer wrestling). They say Bill got mad at a steer one day because he kept turning back while he was trying to pen him, so he jumped off his horse, tipped the steer's nose in the air and locked onto the steer's nose with his teeth, like a bulldog.

The 101 Ranch went bankrupt during the Depression, before my dad was born in 1941. My dad started riding racehorses as a jockey when he was 11, while living with his grandparents. He's spent his lifetime becoming a masterful horseman. He can do amazing things with horses everyone else has given up on. I think that's why I pay attention to every cowboy's horsemanship in every event when I'm at a rodeo. It's a skill I really appreciate, and very few people have mastered it. I enjoy working on my horsemanship, and being a good horseman means a lot to me because I really love horses.

I guess I come by cowboying naturally, because my mom's a hell of a hand, too. She was a two-time world champion girls bull rider in Little Britches Rodeo. And she won the Little Britches world all-around championship in 1956, 30 years to the day before I won it in 1986. She also barrel raced, breakaway roped, pole bended, and competed in the relay and horse races.

My parents got married on Dec. 16, 1961, three days after my mom's 18th birthday. My dad was 20. Dad was breaking 50 horses a year then, dawn 'til dark. They went to amateur rodeos and bull ridings on the weekends, and were so broke they slept in their car. Mom rode her last bull in 1962, when she found out she was pregnant with my sister Kim. Then her kids became her life.

14

Working cattle on the 101 Ranch in Ponca City, Oklahoma. From left to right: My great grandpa Walter Schultz, Chief of Cowboys Jack Brown, unknown, D.H. Farrell, Joe Miller (one of the Miller brothers who owned the 101), unknown, Bill Pickett (the black cowboy who invented bulldogging), my great uncle Guy Schultz (Walter's brother). (Glass Negative photo)

I was born a cowboy. My parents have always said that, and I guess I believe them because that's all I ever wanted to be. I don't ever remember actually stopping to think, "I want to be a cowboy." I've just always felt that way. I never, not even for a day or two, wanted to be the president, a doctor or an astronaut. Rodeo's all I've ever thought about, and I've really loved this sport, everything about it, all my life.

I was born October 11, 1969, and my mom and dad, Butch and Joy Murray, took me home from the hospital in diapers and cowboy boots. My big sisters, Kim and Kerri, and I grew up in Glendale, Arizona, right outside of Phoenix. We lived in a single-wide trailer, and my dad broke racehorse colts for a living. Owners and trainers sent horses to my dad by the semi load because of his reputation for taking on the bad ones and the crazy ones. In the summertime, Dad also worked as a starter at The Downs at Santa

This is where I grew up. Nice looking rodeo rig in the background. (Butch and Joy Murray Photo)

Fe, The Downs at Albuquerque and the Albuquerque State Fair, so for 12 summers we lived in an old adobe house on a racehorse ranch in Piña Blanca, New Mexico.

My dad has always been a cowboy, too. I remember being behind the bucking chutes with him when I was a little bitty kid. I always wanted to be just like him. He taught me more than anyone else about everything, and sometimes he was the best teacher when he wasn't trying to be one. Just watching him and being around him taught me more than any specific lessons I ever learned, and I didn't even realize I was learning at the time.

My dad always did whatever it took to get the job done right — whether he was working or at a rodeo. So he never

had to say, "You've got to try, Ty." I just saw him doing it, so I did it, too.

I started my riding career before I could walk, when I crawled up on the case of my mom's sewing machine. When I was still just a baby, I graduated to the arm of the couch.

As a toddler, I practiced roping every day on my dog, Freckles. I got Freckles when I was born, and roped her all day every day. I swung my rope backwards for a long time, but Freckles didn't seem to care. She was a great dog. When I was tiny, she kept me corralled in the front yard and wouldn't let me wander out onto the dirt road that ran by our house.

When I was a year old I started spending most of my time on an Appaloosa horse we called Doc. Old Doc was a godsend. He was cool. He never got in too big a hurry, and when I tried to get him to do things that would have gotten me hurt or disqualified, he ignored me.

I remember one day when I was barrel racing, and I tried to steer him around the wrong side of a barrel. Doc took care of me and did it right, but I was mad at him until my mom told me he had gone the right way around that barrel. When I was 2, I couldn't remember the cloverleaf barrel racing pattern, so my mom would draw it for me in the dirt and go over it with me right before I rode into the arena. I had no idea what a shrimp I was at the time. I was just a little pee wee, but I thought I could handle anything.

I fell off Doc another day when I was really little. I was convinced it was his fault. So as soon as I dusted myself off, I reached up, grabbed the reins and led him off to the breaking pen to teach him a lesson. I told my parents I was going to "top him off," because I'd heard my dad say that about horses that bucked or ran off.

My mom swears the first words out of my mouth were, "I'm a bull rider." With parents like mine, I don't think anyone was too surprised. I was around a lot of men as a little kid because I spent so much time at the sale barn and racetrack with my dad. So my vocabulary was bigger than I was. One day I ran around the corner of the house chasing Freckles with my rope. My mom was working in the garden. She asked me if I caught Freckles. I told her, "No, Mom, I missed that son of a bitch." After my whipping, I ran down to the breaking pen, where my dad was riding a colt, crying, "Daddy, Daddy! Whatever you do, don't say son of a bitch in front of Mom! She doesn't like it!"

I got on my first calves when I was 2. People assume my parents must have pushed me to ride that young, but that was never the case. They never made me do anything I didn't want to. They let me go as far as they thought I could handle, and probably did let me try a lot more things than most parents do, but they never put me in danger. I loved to ride and they knew it, so they didn't stand in my way.

Because they know I started so young, a lot of people ask me for advice on when I think their kids should start riding. There isn't a perfect age to start, because every kid's different. But before he does start, a kid needs to be strong enough to ride and, more importantly, he really needs to want to ride. I won't let a kid ride at one of my

When I first learned to ride calves, my dad ran alongside to break my falls. Freckles ran out ahead and kept the calves ducking and diving. (Butch and Joy Murray Photo)

schools unless I feel he genuinely wants to get on. When they don't want to do it — when they're doing it to please their parents or impress a girl — is when they get hurt. This sport is way too dangerous to be doing it to impress your girlfriend, to fit in with your friends, or because your dad wishes he'd done it.

I would never suggest that someone stick their 2-year-old on a calf, even though that's what I did. My parents set up a situation that was as safe as it could be, and they knew exactly what they were doing. Most kids don't have that advantage. And the fact is, to be totally safe, a person should never start riding because there's a good chance you'll get hurt even when you do everything right. People have often asked my parents if I ever cried before I got on to ride when I was little. That's almost a joke, because they were the ones who probably felt like crying. I'd beg them to run the calves in "one more time," and they were usually good enough to hold dinner and do it. I couldn't get enough of it, and I had no fear whatsoever. None. I got that from my dad. He was fearless.

When I started riding calves, my dad would run alongside me and hold onto my beltloops. He didn't hold me on, but when I got into trouble he was there to ease my falls and keep me from getting wiped out. He did that 'til I was 4, when I told him I didn't need him anymore.

Back in those early days, Mom counted out eight alligators, then blew a make-believe whistle to let me know it was time to get off. If it looked like I was getting bucked

Old Doc took great care of me when I was a toddler. I worked every event there was on him. (John Crowther Photo)

off early, she counted faster so I'd make the whistle. She was always looking for ways to boost my confidence like that. My parents believed in me so much that I believed in myself. And their personalities really complemented each other. My mom was always there with a "Good try, honey." She told us we could do anything if we tried hard enough. My dad was a little more direct. He praised me more than the law allowed when I did something right. When I messed up he told it like it was. But even when he pointed out my mistakes, he never asked me what *I* did wrong. It was always, "What did *we* do wrong?"

If I had to attribute my success to one thing, it would, without a doubt, be my parents. My mom and dad have always had the greatest influence on my life. I know all parents are important to their kids. But as I get older and look back on my life I realize more all the time just how much they sacrificed for my sisters and me. We were the priority, and everything we did was important to them. Every single decision they made revolved around us three kids. You can't measure love like that, and you can't ever repay it. Lucky for us, seeing us lead happy, successful lives is all the payment our parents need.

I remember always wanting to be good — to tell the truth and go by the rules — when I was a kid. I didn't feel that way because I wanted to avoid being punished, but because I didn't want to disappoint my parents. I loved and respected them so much that I wanted to do right by them, and make them proud of me. I thought they were perfect, and still do, so I didn't want to let them down. That's why I never tried drugs. I respected my parents too much for that. I'd also noticed early on that every single person I ever knew who did drugs regularly was messed up in every way. They never amounted to anything. I saw guys with so much talent go down the tubes, and I thought that was such a waste.

As a kid, riding was my first love. But in my spare time, I was an animal trainer. And I was pretty serious about it. I roped a hog and broke him to ride. I rode him bareback, made a rope halter with a half-hitch around his snout and neck-reined him. I saddle broke a big, black, white-faced bull to ride, too, and heeled steers off of him.

Everything was rodeo — it was the only game I played. I imagined that I was a famous cowboy, and wanted to be just like Larry Mahan. He was the king, in my mind. Back then, when I was looking up to heroes of mine like Larry, Jim Shoulders and Freckles Brown, I set my sights on being the best cowboy in the world. I was willing to work hard, and do

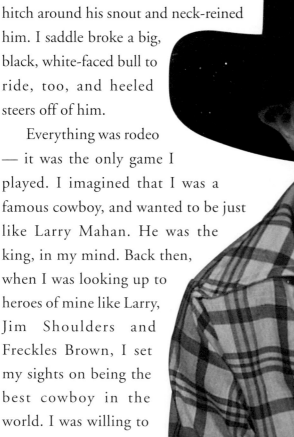

whatever it took to get there. I can remember getting into bed at night and making myself fall asleep with my toes turned out. I tucked the sheets in really tight so they'd hold my feet in that position all night, because I just knew that would make me ride better. Anything to be a better cowboy — that's always been my motto.

When I was 5, I started rodeoing, and by then I was a seasoned veteran in the calf riding. I'd been practicing and working at it for three years. My first rodeo was in Camp Verde, Arizona. There were 20 calf riders, and there was a long round (for everyone entered) and a short round (for the top contestants from the first round). I was the only kid who made the whistle in the first round.

We were tucked in bed in the camper that night after the first day. My dad told me I'd already won the buckle, even though I would ride again the next day. I couldn't understand why they couldn't have just given me the buckle *that* day. At the awards ceremony in the arena the next afternoon they gave me a check for $39, the buckle and a breast collar for winning the all-around. I tried to give them the check back, because I couldn't think of a use for it. All I cared about was that buckle. When they gave me the check back I handed it to my dad and said, "Here, Dad, let's go buy us a Winnebago and a CB."

When I was starting out I went to rodeos every weekend, and practiced one night a week, only because that's the only time they had practice sessions in the area where we lived. I practiced hard until I was a full-time professional, and I'm not too good to practice now. But there are years now when I get on 500 head at the rodeos alone. These days, that's my practice and my competition, and when I "practice" right, they pay me. To actually go to the practice pen now would be taking a bigger chance on getting hurt, especially when I'm tired out from rodeoing. When I'm traveling hard I cherish days off, and use them to give my body a break. If I was a golfer, I'd still practice every day. But in my line of work that'd be suicidal. I now do other things that I think will make me better, like staying in good shape.

People think of me as a roughstock cowboy now. But at 5 years old I wasn't just a calf rider. I was heeling steers horseback and dallying. The saddle I used in those days was so small that my mom has since converted it into a planter. I was so little when I rode it that my stirrups didn't even reach the bottom of the saddle pads.

I was so small when I started chewing Skoal that I had to carry the can in my boot because it was too big to fit in my back pocket. My dad and I used to stay up late, chew and watch Western movies. That was our idea of a great evening. We always watched a lot of rodeo tapes, too. One day when we were hanging out like that, I asked my dad what it felt like to ride a bull that spins. I'll always remember his answer: "It's no different than riding one that bucks straight — he's just going in a circle." That's my dad. He's not one to waste words, or make things more complicated than they really are.

When I was pretty small I'd go into the round pen with my dad, and run Doc in there and knock the buck out of the colts Dad was on. Then we'd laugh. Sometimes we took water guns out there and played cowboys and indians after the work was done. Later, when I was about 8 years old, I used to get on horses at the racetrack that had

bad histories in the starting gate. Because my dad was a starter at the track, he knew which horses had trouble at the gate. He had a reputation for taking on horses that no one else wanted to touch, or other people couldn't handle. Because he was never scared, I was never scared. That helped us get along with horses better than most.

The Murray boys also had a reputation for being wild. Trainers like to gallop horses together, "in company," with their stirrups rubbing each other. My dad and I used to exercise horses like that all the time. If a horse bucked or took off, we just whooped and hollered. We'd get out there early in the morning, when it was so pitch black you couldn't even see the dirt. We were the only ones who rode with cowboy spurs, and we were competitive with each other. To get young horses to break hard out of the gates you're only supposed to go 100 yards and then pull up. We'd vie back and forth for the lead for 400 to 500 yards. God, we had fun.

I've been bucked off more than anyone. I know that for a fact, because in this era, nobody else rides as much as I do. I've worked all three roughstock events since I was 13, and I've been bucked off every way there is — on my back, belly, upside down, on my feet, you name it. I've had the wind knocked out of me, and I've been beaten up so bad I felt like my whole body was broken. I'll never forget the day, at a junior rodeo in Nogales, New Mexico, when I got car-killed in all three events. It was 110 degrees and dusty, and amateur stock bounced me off the fence, slammed me and hooked me. Days like that tested my try and desire, but I always walked away from disappointments even more determined to succeed.

In those early years I went to every horse- and rodeo-related event I could get to. I rode in everything from parades to gymkhanas, which are basically horseback

19

Riding a steer at age 9 with my jaw wired shut at an AJRA rodeo in Tucson. Check out the horn wrap. This is just an old roping steer. (Louise L. Serpa Photo)

Roping on a horse we called Street Car at an AJRA rodeo in Payson, Arizona. This is the "rope and touch" event, where you have to step off, run down the rope and throw your hands in the air to get time. (Louise L. Serpa Photo)

playdays, to junior rodeos. I entered every event at the rodeos, including the barrel race, so I worked hard to be competitive in every event. I never set out to be the best goat tier in the world, but I was competing in it, so I wanted to win. I set the record for the fastest time in that event just because of that determination. I think youth rodeos prepare you for what's coming up in life because you get rewarded for hard work and true dedication. I entered every event at the gymkhanas, too, including the keyhole race, ring grab, flag race and barrel race. I was never much for sitting on the sidelines and watching.

Both my parents went to the junior rodeos with my sisters and I whenever they could. But there were lots of times, especially during the summer racing season, when my dad had to stay home and work so we could afford to go. Even then there were plenty of times he worked all day, drove all night to watch us ride, then drove all night to get back to work. In those days, my mom held $15 back from her grocery money each week to pay our entry fees. I helped out by stomping aluminum cans, too. I even put little rocks in them to make them a little heavier. Anything for entry fees. Even at that age, I loved it. I craved it.

When I was in school we'd leave on Friday nights. In the summertime, we'd leave on Thursday night and get back home Sunday night. One time, when we were driving home from one of those long weekends, I asked, "Mom, don't you wish we were headed to another one like the big boys?" She was about to drop she was so tired, but she said yes anyway.

People talk about "paying your dues" in rodeo. One part of that is spending more time behind the wheel than you do riding, eating and sleeping combined. There are stretches of road — like the drive between Raton and Santa Fe — that bring back old memories of going to all those Little Britches rodeos with my family. We started out in an old, beat-up, green horse van. We'd sweep the manure out of the back, where we hauled the horses, and sleep there.

Then the five of us moved up to a tiny camper. My mom and dad had a bed, and my sisters and I shared a bed. Mom and Dad told us stories before bed every night. After that we had a motorhome. None of it sounds very glamorous now, but when you're a kid it doesn't get much more fun than roughing it a little with your family.

When I decided to start riding bareback horses I spurred a lot of bales of hay to work on my technique and build my confidence. Then my mom would get on a rope horse, dally my horse's (Doc's) lead rope around the saddle horn and pony Doc around. I'd get on him with tennis shoes and practice spurring, trying to make my feet do what I'd seen guys do at the rodeos on TV.

I entered the bareback riding the first time at a little rodeo in Elkhart, Kansas. I was 12 years old, and all I had was a bull riding glove. I'd never been on a bucking horse with my riggin' before — just a bale of hay and Doc. My mom was worried. So we took off on our rope horses right before the rodeo started and rode back into a field behind the arena. Mom tells me we raised a lot of eyebrows. She says everyone was wondering what "the kid and the crazy redhead" were up to. I was too young and nervous to notice or care. The little warm-up session must have helped, because I won the bareback riding that day. I was pretty tickled about that.

Another one of my mom's favorite stories was the time I was in the lead to win a saddle at the Little Britches Rodeo in Woodland Park, Colorado, and all I had to do was make the whistle to win it. Mom told me to mark the horse out and then "d-up," which basically means stick your spurs in the d-rings and just hang on. I would hear none of that, so I didn't take her advice. I spurred the horse out and went to flogging at him for all I was worth. I gave it all I had and got bucked off. She asked me why I did that. I told her if I had to ride with my spurs in the guts I didn't want to ride.

The bareback riding was the hardest of the three roughstock events for me to learn. I didn't begin to ride

21

well in that event until I was 16. I think it took me a lot longer to learn to ride bareback horses than it should have, because I got on a lot of trashy horses when I was just starting out. I think a kid needs to stay in his league when he's learning, and should only challenge himself a step further as his riding progresses. I don't think you should get on anything that's way over your head. Also, it doesn't do you much good just to pick one easy horse or bull and ride him into the ground before moving on. A lot of kids want to do that, but you won't get any better doing it, and you might pick up some bad habits from the lack of variation.

I was small for my age most of the way through school. I went home from school one day when I was in seventh grade and asked my mom if there was something wrong with me. I was only bigger than two other kids in my class, and they had terminal diseases. I was different from all the other kids at my school anyway, because I was a

I was 12 or 13 when this picture was taken on my bucking machine in our back yard. I was just getting ready to start riding saddle broncs. (Butch and Joy Murray Photo)

cowboy, but I was really worried that maybe there was something seriously wrong with me, too. Right after that I had a yearlong growth spurt. I grew three pants sizes and was gangly like a puppy. I had a heck of a time riding, because my body size and coordination were out of whack.

About that time, my parents say I read somewhere about how Harry Tompkins, the great all-around champion from a few decades ago, used to walk a pipe fence to improve his balance. I don't remember reading about it, but I do remember walking the miles of fenceline around that place in Piña Blanca; around all the horse pens and pastures.

I'd be lying if I said the fame and glory part of rodeo didn't fuel the fire a little when I was really young, but I grew out of that pretty fast. As I got older, my love for rodeo came from the actual riding and the independent lifestyle that goes with it. There was nothing I wouldn't do if I thought it might help my riding even a little. I asked for a unicycle one Christmas because I thought it would also improve my balance and coordination. I worked at that thing 'til I could ride it and juggle beanbags my mom made me at the same time. When I really got the hang of it I could rope a (roping) dummy while I rode it. I never thought of that unicycle as a toy. I just wanted to be the best athlete I could be. That's also the reason I took up gymnastics as a kid. I never dreamed of growing up to be the world's greatest gymnast, but I did see a chance to be stronger and more agile, so I took it. I also used to take off riding a horse bareback in the hills every day. Jumping over creeks and logs is great for your balance, too. To be a good cowboy, riding has to be second nature. You have to learn to crawl before you can walk, and you have to learn to ride a broke horse before you can learn to ride an outlaw.

I knew from a young age that there would be sacrifices to make along the way if I was going to get where I wanted to go. I also knew that a little hard work never hurt anyone. My parents showed me that. At one point in my childhood I was getting up at 4 a.m., getting on 15 horses at the track for $5 a head ($10 a head for the bad ones that either bucked or jammed their front feet in the ground, propped and wheeled), taking a shower, going to school, going to gymnastics and wrestling practice, roping 'til dark, doing my homework, going to bed, then getting up at 4 the next morning and doing it all again. Looking back I don't know how I did it. But at the time, my one-track mind wouldn't have it any other way.

When I was 12, I worked for my dad at the track as a flagger at the starting gate. I never spent a dime of what I earned until we got back to Glendale. Then I took that money and bought a bucking machine. We'd stay up 'til 1 in the morning riding that thing. I rode it until my legs were raw and bruised. Then I'd cut up a cardboard box, put it inside my chaps and keep riding. If you ride a bucking machine fundamentally correctly, and don't allow yourself to develop bad habits by always riding it in the same pattern, it can be a good learning tool. There's only so much you can learn on a bucking machine, but there are things you can perfect on one. I think bucking barrels are good at a really early stage, too, for learning the kindergarten fundamentals.

My bucking machine was the centerpiece of our back yard. We set it in concrete and it was surrounded by benches. All the neighborhood kids came over all the time to ride and watch. That bucking machine also turned out to be my ticket to (four-time World Saddle Bronc Riding Champion) Brad Gjermundson's bronc riding school one year. It cost $250 to go to the school. Every time they had an extra $5, my parents stuck it away. But when the school was a week away we were still $60 short. Someone from the school called and asked if I had a bucking machine, and they ended up letting me go to the school for nothing in exchange for using it. I definitely got my money's worth out of that thing.

I went to two of Brad's schools, when I was 15 and 16, and they came at a time in my career when they helped me a lot. I'd been on some horses and could stay on them, but I started really moving my feet at those schools. I got on a lot of horses there, and learned so many little things that have helped me along the way,

like where to place my saddle and the importance of lifting on my rein and setting my feet. I never went to any bareback or bull riding schools, because my dad worked those events. He worked every event but the saddle bronc riding. When he traveled with my mom's brother Butch (the 1980 PRCA World Champion Steer Wrestler) it wasn't unusual for them to win every event at a rodeo between the two of them.

I think rodeo schools are really important in every event. Because when you're a kid and you have several obnoxious, know-it-all dads giving you advice, it's hard to know who to listen to. That's why I wanted to do this book. I was so lucky to have my dad, a teacher I respected, because bad habits are easy to learn and hard to break. After you teach your body to do something one way, it becomes natural to you that way. So if you learn how to do something the wrong way, pretty soon your body just does it like that naturally and it's a long road out.

Good rodeo schools are a cheap investment when you compare them to learning the hard way, from years of experience. I put all of my years of experience, and every world championship I've won, into my schools. When looking for a school, I suggest people pick a cowboy who's about the same size they are. Above that, I suggest you pick the guy you think rides the best and has the best attitude.

Two summers before that first school of Brad's (in 1983 when I was 13) I spent a summer with (six-time PRCA World Champion All-Around Cowboy) Larry Mahan on his ranch in Guffey, Colorado. I was a freshman in high school and was just starting to ride broncs. My dad came home from the sale barn in Glendale one day and said he'd seen Larry at the sale and that he'd asked about me. Dad told him I was starting to ride broncs. Larry said, "Bring him out to the house and I'll help him."

We didn't take him up on the offer because we thought he was just saying that to be nice, as a courtesy. Then Larry called and asked me about my riding, and asked me again

23

Riding one at the National High School Finals Rodeo. (James Fain photo)

to come out. I hung up and off we went. When we got there Larry went and got a really nice palomino cutting horse, and led him into the breaking pen. Then he put my bronc saddle, then me, on him, with nothing on his head. He chased that horse around, and he ducked and dived with me. It was a little wild, but I didn't care. I was still in awe of meeting my all-time hero.

Toward the end of the school year, I got another call from Larry one night. "What are you doing this summer?" he asked me. I told him I was planning on rodeoing. "What would you think about coming and living with me this summer?" he asked.

I didn't know what to think, because I didn't know Larry very well then, and I was just a kid. I didn't want to give up a summer of going to three rodeos a week to go up to Guffey and clean stalls. The work part didn't bother me, but I wasn't wanting to give up valuable rodeo time. I was skeptical, but I decided to take a chance on the chance of a lifetime. I skipped the National High School Finals Rodeo, which was a big deal to me at the time, and headed to Colorado.

What an experience. I broke two colts for Larry that summer. The one colt had eaten loco weed, which makes horses crazy. Larry rode out to him on a paint stud and roped him with a 50-foot rope. Then he snubbed him and blindfolded him with his vest. I jumped on the back of Larry's horse to saddle the colt. We tied two bronc reins together and put them under the colt's neck. I held a rein in each hand, with the reins running around his brisket and no halter on his head.

I'd have jumped off a cliff or fought a bear if Larry'd told me to. That colt took off bucking and spinning. He bucked about 10 seconds, then took off at a dead run. I didn't know if he was going to run through the fence or jump it. About that time, Larry started chasing me around on that stud, trying to rope the colt. He was swinging his rope and it was hitting the colt and slapping me in the face. Then, when Larry got that colt caught and dallied on 20 feet of rope, the two horses ran around opposite sides of a tree. What a wreck.

We started the other colt at Penrose Stadium in Colorado Springs, as a demonstration in front of a crowd. Larry had been asked to be a part of a little exhibition rodeo there. It was a two-part demonstration. First, I was supposed to show the people how bronc riding started. Larry snubbed the colt in the middle of the arena and I got on him. When I did that, the colt spun around and fell over. So much for that part of the demonstration.

Part two amounted to showing the crowd how bronc riding's done today. I rode a bronc out of the chute with a halter and rein. I didn't even know how to ride a bronc then. I'd probably been on five of them ever. But I did all right. I rode him and even moved my feet a little. Larry could've gotten an experienced bronc rider to do the second part of the demonstration, but he purposely put me in that position to test me. I was nervous, but I was gung-ho to do it.

Larry was team roping at the rodeo in Greeley that July. He took those colts for us to ride in the grand entry. Me and another kid named Ben Poer rode to Greeley in the nose of his gooseneck trailer. We had no way of signaling to Larry if we needed anything, so we peed out the little side windows of the trailer.

Larry took me with him everywhere he went that summer, and he was always testing me. He flew us around a lot in his plane. I was the co-pilot. He showed me how to fly it a few minutes and then, without warning, turned the wheel over to me. Then he sat back in his seat, closed his eyes and told me he was going to take a little nap. He just said, "Keep the dash level with the horizon." I'd only been on one or two commercial flights in my life, and had never even sat in a little plane before. I was scared to death, but I never asked any questions. I just did it. But the longer his eyes were closed the wider mine were open. I was so relieved 15 seconds later when he sat up and I realized he was joking that I started breathing again.

One day we flew to an Indian reservation where Larry was going to speak to a camp of delinquent and troubled kids who ranged in age from 12-18 years old. Larry talked to the kids about goals. Then, again without warning, he turned the mike over to me, this little 13-year-old, 80-pound nobody. I said a few words about living in a positive way, and before I knew it those kids were asking me for my autograph.

That summer wasn't a riding school. But I learned a lot from all those little tests. Larry had a plan for everything. I didn't realize it at the time, but now I look back and know he was testing me all the time to see if I was worth my salt.

I was 17 when I went off to college at Odessa (Texas) College, where I had a full-ride rodeo scholarship. I drove out of my parents' front yard in Glendale in an old Ford I bought in high school with money I made galloping horses. I had $700 to my name, and wasn't about to ask my parents for money. I wasn't old enough to join the PRCA (you have to be 18), so I went to amateur and college rodeos. I made an OK living at them — I won a few hundred dollars a week — but couldn't really get ahead. I won something

This was my ride on Oil City Red at the 1988 College National Finals Rodeo. Oil City Red was a famous
NFR horse. That was the year I was the NIRA and PRCA rookie of the year. (James Fain Photo)

about every weekend, but by the time I paid entry fees in three events and paid for my share of the gas, food and hotel rooms, times were tight.

That was a scary time for me. I was 17, and just out of the nest. It was a tough time to see if I could make a living riding. Then again, I never expected it to be easy.

After I lived in the dorm awhile I moved in with Jim Sharp. It was 1988, the year Jim won his first world bull riding championship. Jim was a hero of mine, and is still one of my best friends. We lived in a dive we called the Bronco House. It was an apartment above a saddle shop on Main Street in Odessa, and it was decorated like the "Gunsmoke" days in Dodge City. The way we lived was pretty Western, too. There were take-out boxes on the counter that were growing green things out of them. And in the two years we lived there I never washed the sheets on my bed, which amounted to two mattresses stacked on the floor. Our kitchen table was a cable spool set on end, and there were holes in the walls from wrestling matches and water fights we had with a hose. Our refrigerator was a 1950 model, and it held exactly 10 cases of beer. Not one more can than that, no matter how you stacked them. Believe me, we tried.

I worked all six events (bareback riding, saddle bronc riding and bull riding, steer wrestling, calf roping and team roping) through college. When I turned pro I stuck to the three roughstock events, though I still love to rope. I try to rope every day when I'm home. The older I get, the more I enjoy it. I always try to improve my heading and heeling. I don't think I'll ever get to a point when I think, "I'm good enough — I'll just coast along now." I always try to take it a step further. That goes for my bareback, bronc and bull riding, too.

My true love was always the roughstock events and it showed. I think it'd be next to impossible to rope *and* ride in the roughstock events at the world-class level because of the logistics involved every time you add an event. To haul horses around and stick around for more than one steer at

one rodeo would turn my schedule upside down because of getting split (drawing up in one performance in one event and another performance in another) and having to worry about getting traded (with other contestants if you get up wrong) in yet another event. I really like the timed events, but I love the roughstock events. That difference shows in anything you do.

I've had a lifelong love for animals. I love every kind of animal, especially horses and dogs. They're so smart that they deserve our respect.

I've had a dog since I was born. They're so loyal. I had Freckles until I was 16. Then I had a dog named Boss. He'd ride next to me in the passenger's seat. I'd tell him to hang on and he'd brace himself for the turns. Now I have a dog named Sparky. She's so loyal she'd die for me. She's had a heck of a life. She's been run over, shot, stepped on and kicked by horses.

Five years ago, I ran to the pound to find a dog. I was kind of in a hurry, so I left my truck running. Two hours later, I still couldn't decide which one to take home. So I asked the person working there, "Which one are you going to kill next?" She pointed to Sparky, a mangy little black-and-white mutt who looks like some kind of Aussie/Schnauzer cross. She had a lot of pink skin showing because she was missing so much hair. She'd been shot by a shot-gun in the chest and still has the BBs in her. The Humane Society ended up making T-shirts with a picture of Sparky and I on them and selling them as a fund-raiser.

I keep a few old, retired bucking horses — including Harry Vold's Hermies Worm and No Savvy, who were bare-back horses, and James Harper's Miss KC and Bennie Beutler's Good Times, who used to buck in the saddle bronc riding — in pastures at my ranch. I had Harry's Rusty and Alibi there, too, until they got so old I had to put them to sleep.

This is my dog Bossy. I've always had a good dog. (Murray Family photo)

Hermies Worm (left) and Rusty (right) takin' it easy in their retirement. (Murray family photo)

When Rusty started getting old, Harry started bucking him at college rodeos. I cornered Harry one day and told him I thought the horse deserved better than that. I told Harry I had a pasture full of lush green grass and that I'd spoil him until the day he died. He sent Hermie, too, because he and Rusty always ran together on Harry's ranch. I only drew Hermie once in his career. I had him at the rodeo in Fort Smith, Arkansas, and won the rodeo on him. One day my dad and I were out in the pasture with him at my house. My dad dared me to get on him bareback and boosted me up on his back. He never even quit grazing.

I got No Savvy the same way as Rusty. I'd ridden him several times in his career, and told Harry I'd retire him in style. One day Harry jumped me and said, "God damn it, son, are you trying to put me out of business?" When the horse collicked at El Paso in 1995, Harry called me. I had to leave to get to a rodeo, so I paid a guy to take my truck and trailer down there and bring him back to my ranch.

James Harper sent me Miss KC in 1996, the same year I got Alibi. Miss KC was a great saddle bronc horse. Miss KC and Alibi, who was owned by several stock contractors in his career, were both great broncs. They did so much for so many cowboys and fans over the years. That's why I enjoy sharing what rodeo's done for me with those horses and giving them the royal treatment.

I finally had to put Rusty to sleep when his age took its toll and he started wobbling and staggering. It was a really hard day for me. I had a lot of sentimental feelings about that horse, and in my opinion he was the greatest saddle bronc of all time. I won the 1989 National Intercollegiate Rodeo Association title on him after winning the short round and the College National Finals Rodeo average on him that year. I had to put Alibi down in 1998, and that never gets any easier. I get attached to the old guys and I miss them when they're gone.

BAREBACK RIDING

An hour before the performance starts, I start taking everything out of my riggin' bag. All my equipment is organized by event. I hang my chaps and bull rope up on the fence behind the chutes, and get my bareback riggin' out. I put on my athletic shorts and go to the Justin SportsMedicine trailer to tape up my knees and put on my knee braces. Then I put on my riding pants and boots, and go back behind the chutes. I hang my protective vest on the fence and put the bells on my bull rope. I rosin my riggin' and put on my bareback riding spurs. After everything's set out the way I like it, I start stretching, which is always a really important part of my day at a rodeo.

I'm enjoying myself, visiting with my friends and having fun during all of this, which helps me stay relaxed. I've found that staying relaxed helps me focus.

When my horse is in the chute, the thing I always do first, before he even sees my riggin', is pet him with a calm hand. I go about my business with deliberate moves, without ever being sneaky, because horses can sense fear in a person. I want that horse to sense that I'm not afraid or nervous; that we're both fine and everything's cool. Petting a horse also gives me a chance to get a read on his disposition.

I don't treat every horse the same in the chute. I've been around horses all my life, so I can tell if they're mad or scared, or if they're just old and smart and want to hurt me. If a horse is mad, I do everything I can to get along with him. If he's scared and coiled up like a time bomb, I do everything I can to comfort him. Lots of guys grab a handful of mane and shake

< 1993 Cheyenne Frontier Days Rodeo. I won the short go on Harry Vold's Foxhole.
(Dan Hubbell photo)

Getting ready for my bareback ride in Reno. (Tim Mantoani photo)

it, thinking that'll get a horse used to them. But that doesn't calm a horse. If a horse is old and smart and full of tricks, I take charge in the chute so he reads from my body language that I'm not looking for trouble and don't expect to get any from him, either. I let horses like that know that I'm onto their game, and that I'm not going to play it. We sometimes joke behind the chutes that those old horses are so smart they can hum the national anthem.

After I pet a horse awhile and think I have his disposition figured out, I set my riggin' on him — again deliberately — while standing on the catwalk behind the chute. I use a hook to pull the cinch under his belly, then I pull one side (tighten the cinch) while my helper pulls the other. At that point, I pull it only tight enough to hold it in place if the horse jumps around in the chute. Then I generally

leave the horse alone if he's doing OK and standing in there quietly. If he's young and nervous, I'll spend more time petting him and getting him used to a person touching him.

After my riggin's on the horse, I tape my elbow and wrist. When there are two guys left to ride before me, I put my glove on, and tape it on at the wrist.

Before I tighten my riggin', I make sure everything's straight and in correct position. I want my riggin' sitting on the back side of the slope of a horse's withers — not teetering on the peak — so the front of my riggin's at the actual peak. To tighten the cinch, my helper and I take turns pulling a little each, back and forth. Pulling from both sides keeps the riggin' straighter on a horse's back. It helps me customize the fit to each horse, and also keeps the center of the cinch between the horse's front legs, where it's supposed to be. If you pull too much on one side it can cause your riggin' to be off-center. I like to keep the length of the latigos equal on both sides of a horse, again to keep my riggin' straight on a horse's back.

I never want my cinch tighter than it needs to be, because if it's too tight it might hinder the horse and keep him from bucking as hard as he can. But I don't want my riggin' to come loose, either. That's dangerous and just plain dumb. There might be a lot of mistakes I make in the bareback riding, but my riggin' coming off (which does happen when guys get careless) is not one of them. I pull my cinch tight enough to where I can grab the riggin' and pull it back and forth, and it's tighter than snug.

If a horse is "cinchy," which means he tenses up and holds his breath when he feels the cinch around his belly, I usually try pushing him over to get him a little off balance, which causes him to take some steps and move around in the chute. A lot of times that'll help a horse relax. Cinchy horses tend to stall in the chute, but I've found that I can sometimes help untrack one to where he bucks straight out of there by cinching him up in one chute, then rolling him ahead to the next one.

It doesn't take me long in the chute, and that's the way I like it. Less time in there means less time for something to go wrong and hurt me. When the guy before me finishes his ride, and his horse is headed to the outgate, I start getting on.

Before I make my move onto a horse or bull's back, I put my foot on his back so he knows I'm coming. Animals get distracted by all the same things we do — the clowns, the band, and whatever's going on in the arena. I want to get his attention back on me, so I don't scare him.

Before I sit on a bareback horse, I stand above him and get my bind, with my feet pointing straight ahead so a horse won't catch my spurs if he jumps. While I'm standing over a horse getting my hand in the riggin', I lean to the right a little, because I'm right-handed and

don't want my body on one side and hand (stuck in the riggin') on the other if I do end up in a storm. That way, if a horse rears up or flips, I can get off to the right and out of his way in one quick move.

Simply put, "the bind" is the way the glove fits in the riggin' to help you hang on. To get my bind, I put my hand in the riggin' to the center of my palm, behind my callouses. Then I crack the front of my hand out slightly, which locks the knuckle of my index finger on the edge of the front of the riggin'. I then close my hand, and straighten my wrist and hand to a natural position. The actual bind is around the base of the pinky and at the base of the index finger, where the outside edges of my hand meet the riggin'.

Once I get my bind, I sit on my riggin' and put my feet, pointing forward, on the slats on each side of the chute. I don't jump or ease down on the horse; I just sit down on him with the same calm, deliberate body language I've used since first walking up to him.

I rest my free arm on top of the back of the chute or gate, depending on the "delivery," which refers to which way the gate opens. At most rodeos, half the chutes face each direction, so half of them open to the left and the other half open to the right. Stock contractors load their horses and bulls for the delivery that suits their bucking style. If a horse tends to buck in a circle to the right on his right lead, for example, they'll load him for a right-hand delivery so when he leaves the chute he's already on that lead. If a horse or bull that likes to buck on his right lead is loaded for a left-hand delivery, he'll usually take a stutter-step or a little run to switch to the lead he likes before he starts bucking. So basically, they load horses and bulls so they can buck their best straight out of the chute.

33

The two keys to bareback riding are lifting on your riggin' and setting your feet. If you do those two things, you have a chance. If you don't, you're done.

I leave the chute with my riding arm straight, lifting as hard as I can on my riggin', with my riding arm in the same position I'm going to ride in. The only way a horse can jerk my butt off my riggin' is if he tears my arm off. I ride with my riding arm basically straight because there's going to be a point in every jump — when a horse peaks and breaks over — where a horse will jerk it straight anyway.

I'll nod for a horse if he's down in front, in back or flat on his belly, squatting or sprawled out with his head down, as long as the flankman can get the flank. The only exception is if he's leaning so hard that I can't get my legs in position, or if he's looking back into the chute. If a horse is looking back into the chute he doesn't know the gate's open. He's more likely to rake you off on the gate or come out of there backwards.

I nod for horses that aren't standing perfectly in the chute because a horse has to get up before he can buck. I

On Cotton Rosser's Manzanita Moonshine at the 1994 NFR. (James Fain photo)

also do it because stock contractors appreciate cowboys who help their show roll along. Contestants can help or hurt themselves by making the best of tough situations. If a horse gets out (before you nod) or falls down while he's bucking, the stock contractor has the option of bringing him back or running in the reride horse. Fred Dorenkamp brought back his best horse for me one year at Kansas City because he knew I'd tried hard to make it work.

I nod for a horse with my feet on the chute slats on each side of the horse, back by the cinch. That gives me momentum for my spur-out. I don't drop my feet down to mark a horse out until he starts to leave the chute. Then I reach forward with my feet. I place my spur shanks in front of a horse's neck with my calves into his neck. Turning my toes out helps take away any doubt in the judges' minds about my spur-out. It not only looks better, it also helps me hold my feet because the shanks of my spurs are in front of the horse's neck.

There's never an excuse for missing a bareback horse out, because marking one out is simple. The only exception is something so bad that it would get you a "free roll" anyway, because you were fouled. For example, if a horse runs down the gate and you can't physically get your feet up where they're supposed to be, the judges will yell, "Free roll" or "Go on," which lets you know they've waived the mark-out rule.

Right when a horse commits himself, I make a quick, snappy placement of my feet, so they're set before the horse's front feet first hit the ground. I don't do it before he commits himself, because I don't want to throw my feet up there when a horse is stalled in the chute. That would be asking for trouble, and might scare him into flipping over backwards. But while a horse is actually committing himself, he's thinking about what he's doing and won't hardly even notice my feet. I watch a horse's head and ears because they tell me when he's going to commit himself and where he's headed.

I like to keep my feet up there where they're supposed to be for the spur-out — at the point of the break of the shoulder on each side — for two jumps. I do that for two reasons: 1. I think it gets me off to a better start because I give a horse a chance to really start bucking before I start spurring, basically setting up a more successful ride; and 2. The spur-out rule says you have to mark one out for one jump, but two is safer because of some of the moves horses throw you before they start bucking, like half-jumps, stutter-steps, scoots and skips. Those moves can fool me or the judges if I'm not on the safe side.

The starting position for each jump is with both feet set up at the front as the horse extends. If a horse runs before he starts bucking, I want my feet set in the neck until he breaks. Then, when he takes that first jump, the momentum throws everything back — my head and my feet. As the horse peaks and breaks over, that momentum changes again, which gives me a chance to bring my head and feet back down and set them again before the next jump. After the second jump, when a horse comes up with his front end and pushes off with his hind legs, that's when he "sends me my feet," or gets a blast of energy behind my spur stroke.

By the time my feet get back to the handle of the riggin' at the end of each spur stroke, the horse'll be starting to peak just before heading back down to the ground. As he peaks and breaks over, I want to bring my head back down to see my feet set back in front of the shoulders when the horse is fully extended, just before the horse hits the ground again. I want my feet to pause there in that set position for a split second while the horse extends and comes back to the ground. Then I'm back in the starting position and ready for the next jump.

When people talk about "exposure" in the bareback riding, they're talking about how wide open you are with your legs. Faster bucking horses allow you less exposure, because you have to come straighter and quicker back down

35

with your feet to start each spur stroke to stay in time with them. A stronger horse that hangs longer each jump gives you time for more exposure; to come out farther with your feet before coming back down, which looks flashy. But regardless of a horse's speed or style of bucking, I always want my feet set before a horse hits the ground with his front feet again.

When a horse really bucks, his front end's still off the ground when he's kicking. Then he has to drop down even more with his front feet. I use my feet to keep me centered on a "droppy" horse. When my feet are set, I'm lifting on my riggin' and I'm leaned back, I have stability; I'm locked in. Doing those three things keeps me square and from whipping forward or moving from side to side. If both of my feet are set, I can't get whipped forward and that

This is a good example of spooning, where my feet are getting whipped back. (Murray Family photo)

horse can't get me off my riggin'. And when I'm leaned back, my feet are light. They're easier to move up or down, so I can place them where I want them. I also have greater range of motion for my spur stroke. I never move my body forward with a bareback horse, I just resist his forward motion with my feet.

I try to watch my feet set every jump, when the horse kicks in back and extends. My head gets snapped back every jump, but I keep bringing it forward to see my feet set, at the start of each spur stroke.

If I get tipped off to one side, I use both feet to get squared back up again. If I'm getting whipped to the right, I want to keep reaching and spurring with my left foot and using my right foot as a brake when I set it as the horse kicks. As the horse jumps, I want my right foot to come

back to the riggin' extra hard on the next jump, so that momentum will help push my body back to the middle and square me up. When I am square, I want my feet setting and coming to me evenly. If I keep my body square, my feet will stay even, and vice-versa.

A bareback riding spur stroke starts in front of a horse's neck and then comes up the neck with each jump. I like to get ahold of a horse's neck with the calf of my leg, then roll the spur up his neck to try to help me pull against all the momentum that's going away from me. I try to bring my feet to my handle with my toes turned straight out while keeping my knees in.

The reason I roll my spurs up a horse's neck is to get some drag and pull as the horse's momentum is going away from me during the jump; so my feet aren't just whipping back to me. Rolling my spurs gives me control because of the constant contact with the horse, and keeps the riggin' from getting jerked away from me. It also helps me with my timing, so I can keep my feet in the right place at every point in a ride. And if I'm clubbing a horse in the neck — chopping at him instead of gliding my spurs up his neck — he's not going to buck as hard.

"Spooning" is a common spurring mistake made in bareback riding. You're spooning when your feet are out of control and whipping back to your d-rings or latigos. It happens when you're trying to spur and get behind, usually when you're sitting up too straight and taking jerks. That causes your feet to whip back instead of rolling back to your riggin'. To prevent spooning, keep your body position far enough back to allow you to expose yourself and reset your feet.

Spurring one in Colorado Springs. This is right after the horse has peaked, broken over and started to kick. My feet are even. Now I need to get my chin and feet back down. (David Jennings photo)

I like to think of my free arm as a pilot. When a bronc or bull throws me a move that gets me off balance, I move my free arm where I want to be and my body follows. If my body gets tilted to the left, for example, I move my free (left) arm over to the right and it squares me back up. A lot of guys tuck their free arms in close to their bodies when they leave the chute. As soon as the gate opens, I hold mine at a 90-degree angle to start off with, because that's a neutral place to keep it until I need it for balance. Then I put it where I need it, which is easy from that 90-degree base position.

In my eyes, the ultimate sin in bareback riding is double-grabbing. It is never acceptable. The reason I feel so strongly about it is because when you're double-grabbing you're not trying to fix the problem. And if you double-grab every time things get hairy, you develop a terrible habit, and will never win. Success at anything you do in life depends on how bad you want it, and how hard you go at it. In most cases, double-grabbing is nothing but a sign of weakness and lack of heart.

My feet are set, my body's square and I'm ready for the next jump at the National Western Stock Show and Rodeo in Denver. (Dan Hubbell photo)

◄ Catchin' serious air. This horse is still jumping, and my feet are almost set. This horse jumped so high he gave me a lot of time to set my feet before he hit the ground again. 1990 California Rodeo in Salinas. (Fred Nyulassy photo)

When the whistle blows, I grab the front of my riggin' with my free-arm hand. That gives me something to hold on to while I work my hand out. To get my riding hand out of the riggin', I open it, lean forward with my elbow down, jerk my hand forward and back once each and I'm out. After the whistle is the only time I lean forward in the bareback riding. At that point my bind is broken and I'm just holding on by squeezing the handle.

It's important to keep riding in time with a horse after the whistle. When he jumps, you need to lean forward to counteract his forward motion. When he kicks, you need to lean back to counter his dropping momentum.

If a horse is still bucking it's pretty easy to use the pickup man. It's a lot harder when a horse is just running off, because you have no momentum to help pop you up over the pickup horse's butt. You want to try to get off behind the pickup man. I reach to grab his hip or the back of his saddle and try to grab him low, and not around the neck or shoulders, so I don't jerk him off his horse. Of course, when I'm in a bind I have to grab for whatever I can get. But if the pickup man falls off on me, and both horses run over us, it's not good for either of us. It's important to cooperate with a pickup man because he's there to help you.

When possible, I want to get all the way over the pickup horse's butt, and get down on the ground on the other side, to avoid getting kicked by the bucking horse, dropped, and run over. As I make my move over onto the pickup horse I draw up my legs, get my shins up on the bucking horse's back, and push off with my legs.

After the bareback riding, I take my glove and neck roll off, then I take the tape off of my elbow and wrist, and take off my chaps and tail pad. I keep stretching as I take off all my bareback riding gear and start getting ready for the bronc riding.

Here's a pretty good example of the right way to get off on a pickup man. (PRCA photo by Dan Hubbell)

There's an old rule of thumb about choosing which hand to ride with. It says that if you're right-handed you should ride with your left hand so you can use your dominant hand or free arm for balance. I disagree. You'll learn balance either way, so it makes sense to me to use your strongest hand to hold on with. I ride with my right hand because it's my dominant hand — I eat with it, write with it, play tennis with it and zip my pants with it — so it's stronger. But that's just my personal preference. I feel like I could've learned to ride with either hand.

There are great champions in every event that ride with each hand. That tells me that it doesn't matter which hand you ride with; that you should forget about what everybody else thinks, and go with whatever feels best to you.

Rodeo equipment's cheap. It's nothing next to all the other expenses of rodeoing, so it's well worth it to spend the extra money and get the best. You can pay for the difference in price at one rodeo by winning more. A cheap piece of equipment can cost you a lot more than the difference in price, and is potentially dangerous.

I have a reason for every piece of equipment I use. I don't use anything because "that's the way it's always been done." I believe in everything I use and why.

I carry a clothes bag, briefcase, bronc saddle and riggin' bag with me wherever I go when I'm rodeoing. So while I never want to be caught without everything I need, I have to pack efficiently. And because I keep the tools of my trade — everything I need to work all three events, including my bareback riggin', bull rope and chaps — in my riggin' bag, I want it to be strong and waterproof.

It's important to get good equipment and to make sure it fits you correctly and suits your level of riding. But once you get the basics covered, it's just as important not to use your equipment as an excuse. I never blame my equipment if I don't make a good ride. I never blame a bad ride on anything else, either. A lot of guys beat themselves — even at the National Finals Rodeo level — because they get too technical and scientific about things. They worry about little minor adjustments that really don't matter and second-guess themselves right out of the money. I also never let an animal that doesn't buck very hard affect my riding or how I adjust my equipment, because I want everything adjusted so I can ride one that really bucks.

I don't care if it's raining, snowing or 115 degrees, get tough and ride with everything you've got. I never let the rain or mud bother me, and I don't worry about what it might do to my equipment. I take a shower every morning and live through getting wet every time. If my rope or saddle or riggin' get wet, who cares? Weather is just another meaningless excuse.

A bareback riggin' is made of leather, rawhide and neoprene, which makes the center core and helps the body last longer. In the body of the riggin', there's rawhide only in the peak, which is the highest point in the arch of the riggin'. The rawhide on both sides of the peak keeps the peak from flattening out when the cinch is pulled tight. The leather in the body of the riggin' allows it to comfortably fit a horse's back and withers. A good cowboy worries as much about how his riggin' or saddle fits a horse as how it fits himself.

I ride with a riggin' that has an all-rawhide handle (or handhold) except for one piece of leather that runs down the left side of the top of the handle. I like the body of my riggin' to be stiff so it won't roll from side to side during a ride.

The handle of my riggin' splits into two bars. I like the right bar to go under the body of the riggin', and the left bar to run over the body of the riggin'. A lot of guys have both bars under the peak to bring it up more, further toward them. I don't like that because the torque — or natural momentum — always pulls away from your riding hand. So because I ride with my right hand, I have one bar on top of the peak on the left side. That bar acts as a brace and prevents my handle from twisting over to the left. I want my handle to sit directly over a horse; so the handle's at dead center over his back.

A lot of bareback riders have been big on having their riggins set up and tilting toward them the last few years. Some guys even use clamps when their riggins are in their gear bags to squeeze their peaks together. The only place their riggins touch a horse is just above the d-rings. Those guys think that helps them keep their riding elbows bent. But those riggins don't comfortably fit a horse, and that's not in a cowboy's best interest. A horse needs to be comfortable in order to perform his best.

I like to find a happy medium with my peak. If it's too wide and sits too flat, a horse can work my hand out of the handle easier because my hand and wrist get extended too far, and it overextends/hyperextends my elbow. If it's set up too far, it feels like it's in my face and I don't have anything to lift from so I can get on tilt too easily.

With a happy medium in the body of my riggin', my wrist isn't turned up or down. It keeps me square, because my wrist is in a natural position. My riggin' fits 99 percent of the horses I get on comfortably; all of them except horses with extremely steep or flat withers.

My bareback riggin'. (Kendra Santos photo)

Some guys go through three or four riggins a year. I'll use a riggin' three or four years. I buy the best equipment and take care of it, because once I get it right I want it to last. I use the same riggin' until it starts to break down and pull flat.

When you order a riggin' you need to specify your hand or glove size. I've also traced my hand on a piece of paper for a riggin' maker to keep on file. It's important for the guy making your riggin' to have an exact measurement from the outside of your pinky to the outside of your index finger, taken across the base of your fingers, in order to get the handle size right. You also need to state your bar preferences when ordering a riggin'.

I use a Barstow riggin', model PR 94, handle size $9^1/_2$. I think Barstow riggins (Corsicana, Texas) are by far the best on the market because they're built to last the longest and fit a horse the best. Their quality and size is so consistent that if I had one shipped straight to a rodeo I'd have confidence that it'd be exactly the same as the last one.

When I get a new riggin' I modify it to fit me exactly. It's important to read the PRCA rulebook before making adjustments to your equipment to be sure everything you do is legal. An adjustment isn't an advantage if you get disqualified for it or it's unsafe, but getting your riggin' to fit you just right is critical in bareback riding.

The hand space in the riggin' (measured from the top of the peak to the under side of the handle) is standard. I personalize it with a piece of leather that I glue to the top side of the top of the peak; right under the handle.

National Western Stock Show and Rodeo in Denver (1994). This is what happens when your hand comes out of the riggin'. It's the most dangerous thing that can happen. (Dan Hubbell photo)

I file the edges off the top of the handle leather and rawhide to smooth the corners. I also file off the corner edge of the bar that's on top of the peak. I file off all rough edges that come in contact with my hand during a ride and after the whistle, when I'm jerking my hand out of the riggin', because I need to do everything I can to protect my hand. It's hard to keep my riding hand from getting sore even when everything's just right, and it's no fun to ride with a sore hand.

If my riggin' doesn't feel just right, I put it on a gentle saddle horse to run my hand in it, crack it back and see how it feels. I work on it 'til it feels perfect, then leave it alone. When I get to a rodeo I don't keep running my hand in my riggin' to see how it feels. I never run my hand in the handle unless it didn't feel good on the last horse and needs to be adjusted. All that does is wear my glove out and make my hand sore.

The pad used under a riggin' is important because it covers and protects the pressure point on a horse's back, where the riggin' touches him. I use a high-density foam pad that's covered with chap leather, with saddle leather sewn on the pressure point at the back of the riggin'. It serves as a shock absorber and disburses the pressure on a horse's backbone, so he's comfortable throughout the ride.

I use the widest cinch I can find — it's nine inches wide — because that also helps disburse the pressure of the riggin'. When it comes to cinches, the wider the better. I pull my cinch with it positioned right behind the horse's front legs, and use long, nylon latigos because they're easy to pull.

I like my bareback riding gloves thick but somewhat supple. The thickness offers better protection and helps them last longer. Shawn Schild (Blackfoot, Idaho) makes my gloves, which are size 9 1/2, out of cowhide.

I also make adjustments to my bareback riding gloves before I use them. I take a razor blade and remove the ridged stitching that runs along the index finger. I then baseball stitch it back together to make a flat, comfortable seam.

Then I split my glove at the center of the top of my wrist, half an inch beyond the break of the wrist. I overlap it and tape it on my wrist for a snug fit with no bunching.

I cut the tip out of the thumb of my glove, because when I pull it on and close my hand it makes the thumb of the glove feel too short. It gives me more movement with my thumb, which makes it easier to wrap my thumb around the handle. It also moves the palm piece down where it should be, running from along the base of my fingers down to the base of my pinky.

The leather palm piece I glue inside my glove makes the corner on the pinky side and wraps around the end of my hand. The palm piece creates the bind that helps me hold on to my riggin'. I like to get most of my bind at the base of my pinky, and want to feel like I'm holding on to my handle, though it's actually holding on to me. I want my riggin' to feel like I'm squeezing it; not like my hand's stuck in it.

Taping my glove on at the Reno Rodeo. (Tim Mantoani photo)

I glue a pad inside my glove to protect the back of my hand. It runs down the top of the index finger over the top knuckle. With the pad, my hand doesn't bang against the front of the riggin' when I pull my hand out of the handle after the whistle. I also paint tincture benzoin, which you can get at any drugstore, on the palm of my glove, across the area where I get callouses at the base of my fingers. It makes the leather harder and stiffer, and helps me get a better bind. I paint a thin coat of tincture benzoin on both sides of the glove, let it dry, and apply a few more coats.

There's no way I can ride up to par with today's style — reared back, gapped open, ripping both feet back to the handle — without the handle actually holding on to me. And I don't want my hand to come out when my body's in the laid-back position it has to be in to ride right. If your hand comes out there's a good chance of getting kicked in mid-air or landing on the back of your head.

In the old days, they sat up straighter and rode with "rag" (leather) handles that they actually had to hold on to. I wish it was a rule that everyone had to do that today, because I don't think bareback horses have a chance to buck very many guys off the way the riggins are now. If everyone rode with a rag handle, the best cowboys would definitely win, because you couldn't get away with just locking yourself in there.

Even today, I think it's important for a guy who's learning to ride to hold on to the handle with nothing but his grip while he's getting a feel for horses. He doesn't need to be bound to his riggin' until he rides good enough for that to be safe. I started riding bareback horses when I was 12, but didn't get a bind until I was 16, because my dad wanted me to learn to ride before I locked myself in. I think that's a good idea for everyone.

Once you've mastered a softer handle and the basics of riding, you can graduate to a riggin' that's half rawhide, then to one that's all rawhide. I started riding with an all-rawhide riggin', because that was all we had, and rode with it until Larry Mahan gave me one that was half-and-half. It was a lot better for me at that stage of the game, and that's what I recommend to beginners if they can't find a rag handle.

I use black rosin, the kind you can get from any rodeo supplier, in all three events. I use the same rosin in all three events just to keep things simple. Yellow rosin's also available, but like a lot of other things it just comes down to personal preference. I use rocks of rosin in the bronc riding and bull riding, and broken up rocks of rosin inside a sock that make a powder in the bareback riding. In the bareback riding, the powder acts like baby powder and helps me slide my gloved hand into the handle of my riggin'. In the other events, the rosin's tacky so it gives me extra grab.

My bareback riding spurs. (Kendra Santos photo)

I like my bareback riding spurs to be straight-shanked; not angled inward. Mine have a two-inch shank with a half-inch drop. In the bareback riding you want your spur to start each stroke in front of a horse's neck; not in the neck. I like a bareback riding spur shank to drop slightly because I don't want it to stick straight out and poke a horse like a prong.

The band (the part that goes around the back of the boot) on my bareback and bronc riding spurs is an inch wide. On my bull riding spurs it's an inch and an eighth. Basically, the rule of thumb on spurs is that they need to be heavy enough so they won't bend.

I use a four-point, squared-off, dull rowel in the bareback riding. I ride with the dullest spurs in the PRCA, because I don't ever want to hurt an animal or hinder his performance in any way. The spurs I ride bareback horses with are trophy spurs from the 1989 rodeo in Clovis, New Mexico. Sam Jenkins (Texico, New Mexico) made them. Coincidentally, he made my first pair of spurs for me when I was six months old.

I use baling wire or a coat hanger for my heel strap, which helps hold a spur in place, because I'm always walking around in dirt, manure and mud, which rot leather. I like wire, because the way things usually go, if a leather strap's going to break, it's going to break on a good horse for a lot of money; not on a dink. I put tape around the wire to protect my boot and keep the wire from digging into it. The tape also takes up slack to make a perfect fit.

I do, however, use a leather spur strap. Spur straps are thick enough and wide enough not to break, and they don't rot because they run across the front of your boot and don't come in contact with the ground. Most guys tie their boots on in the bareback riding by taking several wraps around the tops with a long leather thong. That works OK. But I use a leather strap with a buckle on it because that's all I need and it's quicker for me, which is a consideration when you work three events.

I like to use leather instead of things like wire and nylon whenever possible because leather is strong enough that it won't just break for no reason. But it will break if it has to. If my spur catches on something, leather will break before it tears my leg off.

I use the same boots in all three events. They're black, square-toed 7 1/2 EEs. The toe is just a personal preference. I want a strong shank in my riding boot — mainly for saddle bronc riding — because it helps the stirrups feel consistent throughout each ride, and from ride to ride. I want the heel to be high enough so it won't let my foot slip through a stirrup, but low enough not to increase my chances of twisting an ankle when I jump off after a ride or run back to the chutes. My boots have 13-inch tops, which gives me plenty of space to tie them on in the bareback riding and bull riding, and added protection for my shins.

I use shin guards in all three events. The ones I use are made by Sondico and are designed for soccer. They provide shin and ankle protection, and are so comfortable I don't even know I have them on.

White athletic tape is a key piece of preventive equipment in the roughstock events. It's especially important for my wrist and elbow on my riding arm. Because I've had knee injuries, I use three-inch elastic tape with pre-wrap under it on my knees. Under the pre-wrap I use a spray-on tape adherent for a sticky, non-slip base.

Tape is only effective when it's used correctly, and I don't use it to make me ride better. I use it to prevent injuries and keep from getting sore. I tape my own ankles, knees and wrists so I can do it consistently. A team doctor doesn't follow me around, and I want everything to feel the same every time I ride. Dr. J. Pat Evans of the Justin SportsMedicine

Team taught me to tape my wrist. Justin's Bill Zeigler showed me how to tape my knees. Lewis Field (a three-time world champion all-around cowboy and two-time world champion bareback rider) taught me how to tape my elbow. Cody (Lambert) and I invented our own way of taping our hands in the bull riding.

I don't suggest that anyone tape his own knees or ankles unless he's been taught by a doctor or qualified trainer, because doing it wrong can be more harmful than not doing it at all.

I only use a neck roll in the bareback riding, and the one I use is homemade. I take a cotton tube and fill it with a rolled-up towel. The ones they use in professional football are good, but they connect to shoulder pads, which I don't wear. The cotton tubing I use is long enough so the part with the towel in it runs around the back of my neck, then the cotton tubing crosses in front of my neck, crosses again in back and ties in front. I use the neck roll for whiplash prevention. It stops my head from snapping too far back when I'm getting jerked each jump.

The tail pad I wear under my jeans is made of high-density foam, and is half an inch thick. I wear it to protect my tail bone and crotch. Most tail pads are almost a perfect circle. I cut mine with an extension on one side to run up the front of my jeans, right along the zipper. A little extra protection never hurt a guy. Tail pads last forever. I used the same one from when I was 12 until I was 25, and then made a new one. It'll probably last me the rest of my career.

A lot of cowboys only wear a protective vest in the bull riding. I use one in all three events. Without one in the bareback riding, the quick-release buckle on a flankstrap gouges my back and rips my shirts when I lay back to spur. I think a vest is a good idea in all three roughstock events, because it also gives me basic protection if I was to get kicked, stepped on or hit, or flipped on in the chute. Cody came up with the first protective rodeo vest, and his is the one I wear because it's the best vest out there. Cody was the only guy who wore a vest at the 1993 NFR. Now everyone wears one in the bull riding, and I think you're crazy if you don't because they prevent all kinds of internal, back, rib and collarbone injuries.

More and more guys are wearing them in the other riding events, too. Protective vests are mandatory in all three roughstock events in some of the youth rodeo associations, and I think that's great. A lot of guys are walking away from wrecks that would have hurt or killed them before the vests came out. Since they don't hinder your performance at all, I can't imagine a good reason not to wear one.

Chaps provide protection and flair in the roughstock events. My chaps have three straps that fasten around each leg. I have a piece of leather sewn on where the swells of the saddle hit my leg in the bronc riding. It acts as another pad because that spot is twice as thick. It helps disburse the pressure of the swells, and helps my chaps last longer.

I like my chaps long enough to go right to the ground, but don't want them to touch the ground so I won't step on them and trip when I'm running to get to safety or climbing the fence.

My dad made my chaps when I was little. They were black with white trim and had three teardrops down the side, just like his. From 1990 on, I've had the same buckskin-colored chaps with baby-blue trim. I wore turquoise chaps at my first NFR in 1989, but since 1990 I've worn buckskin and baby blue. When I bought my first pair of chaps when I was 15 they were exactly like the ones I wear now. I wanted to ride my whole career with the same kind of chaps. I remember watching (14-time National Finals Rodeo bull rider) Wacey Cathey in rodeo films when I was a kid. You could spot his trademark green chaps with the dollar signs down the legs even if you couldn't see his face. I thought that was pretty neat.

I picked baby blue for my trademark color because it's been my favorite color since I used to drag a baby blue blanket around through the dirt and manure in our arena at home when I was little. I wouldn't give that thing up, so my mom cut a corner off of it every day until it was gone.

Sterling Lamb (Billings, Montana) makes my chaps. I wear them loose in the bareback riding because I'm not holding on with my chaps, and that way my legs are freer to spur. I wear them tighter in the saddle bronc riding because my legs are up against the swells and I don't want my chaps rolling around on my legs. I wear my chaps loose in the bull riding because that's what's comfortable in that event.

When my chaps get muddy, I use water and a plastic brush to clean them up. Then I use saddle soap or saddle butter as a leather conditioner. Cody always makes fun of me about how meticulous I am with my equipment. But that equipment is what I make my living with. Keeping everything clean, dry and conditioned, from my spur straps to my saddle, just makes good sense to me.

I always carry a pair of riding jeans in my riggin' bag (Wranglers, size 31 X 36 — a size bigger since I started wearing knee braces under them). I do that because if I didn't take off my riding pants and put on clean ones, most restaurants and airlines wouldn't let me through the door.

I wear supportive sports shorts under my jeans. They basically work like a girdle when I ride. They keep my hip, butt and groin muscles warm and compressed, and really make a big difference in preventing my groin and hamstring muscles from getting sore and torn.

The sheepskin-lined flankstrap used in all three roughstock events is provided by the stock contractor. It's made so no metal from the buckles ever comes in contact with a horse or bull. The flankman pulls the flank as the horse leaves the chute. The length or tightness is preset for each animal so the flankman just has to pull a leather strap. It's important that the flankstrap is the right length — loose enough to where the animal thinks he can kick it off and tight enough so it won't come off during the ride.

47

SADDLE BRONC RIDING

Saddle bronc riding is about trying to make a perfectly flawless ride with finesse, grace and snap. After I get my bareback riding equipment put away, I put my chaps back on, put the rein on my halter and set my halter, rein and bronc saddle on the ground. When I put my rein on the halter I loop it through so the rein comes up through the loop instead of down. Having the rein come back up through the loop keeps the rein up away from my feet a few extra inches during each spur stroke, which makes it that much harder to spur over my rein because the rope isn't sagging down. I never want to spur over my rein because when that happens, there's a chance I'll hang a spur, which'll throw my timing off. On a bucker, it'll get me thrown off.

I rosin my chaps in the saddle bronc riding for the same reason I rosin my saddle; so the swells of my saddle won't be slick. I don't want my chaps or saddle to be sticky, but do want enough rosin on there to keep the leather from being slippery. I rosin my chaps and saddle at the same time before each ride, after first removing the old dirt and rosin with a wire brush. To apply new rosin, I sit in my saddle on the ground and put little rocks of rosin between the saddle and the part of my chaps that comes in contact with it. Then I break and grind the rosin into the swells of the saddle with my legs while pulling the fork of the saddle up and down with both hands. The heat caused by that friction melts the rosin and works it in, and gives me the amount of "grab" I'm looking for.

Once that's done, I get up on the chute — just me — without any equipment. I pet my horse with a calm, deliberate hand and talk to him with a steady voice. I'll say, "Whoa" if he jumps or gets nervous in there, but don't let my voice get excited if the horse docs. No matter what he

< The jump from the dirt to the grass at the Pendleton Round-Up. (Richard Roschke photo)

does, I never change my tone of voice or manner of moving around. I'm always calm. I might ask a horse, "You doing OK today?" And tell him, "I'm doing good." What I'm basically doing in a friendly voice is giving that horse the idea that, "This guy's been here before and he's not worried. This must not be any big deal."

Common sense works with horses. I always put myself in their shoes. I think it's fun to try to get along with horses and understand them. I pride myself in that. I never want a horse to respect me out of fear. I'm also never sneaky around one. Coyotes are sneaky, and that's the reason people don't like them and other animals don't trust them.

The first thing I put on a bronc is my halter. I stand on his left side — the buckle side — to do it because it keeps me from having to reach over his head, and makes it easier to buckle and adjust the halter. I position myself back by the horse's withers when I'm putting the halter on, so if he throws his head up he won't hit me in the nose. I drop the halter down in front of his shoulders, then reach over his neck and get the strap with my right hand while keeping the buckle in my left. Then I slowly move forward to the horse's head, and slide the halter on, again deliberately. I adjust it to where it fits the horse's head snug, because I've seen horses buck halters off.

While I'm putting the halter on a horse, I keep the tail of the rein on my side of the chute, between the chutegate and my hip, so it won't fall in the chute and scare him or give him something to paw at.

Once the halter's on the horse's head, I take the rein —

Wire brushing the old rosin off my chaps before a bronc ride. (Tim Mantoani photo)

back by his withers again — in my left hand and ease it under his brisket. I reach over the horse's withers with my right hand to pull the rein through, and lay it over his neck. I don't tuck my rein into the halter up by his eyes and ears like some guys do, because I give broncs as few reasons as possible not to like what I'm doing, and those are sensitive parts on a horse.

Then I pet the horse some more. I like to see a horse lick his lips, blink his eyes or take a deep breath, like a sigh, because those are signs he's relaxing.

When I put my saddle on, I try to make all my adjustments from above the horse. I don't stick my arms through the boards or bars of the chute because that's a good way to break them if a horse jumps around in there.

I don't decide where to place my bronc saddle by where it sits on a horse's back, because that's not as important as where my stirrups hit a horse when they're pushed forward, in position for a spur stroke. I start pulling the front cinch of my saddle with a full stirrup's length in front of a horse's neck. As I pull it tight, it settles back to where there's about half a stirrup's length ahead of the horse's neck, which is the length I need in order to set my feet in front of the neck for the spur-out and the rest of the ride. That position adjusts for the length of my legs based on the length of my stirrups, and explains why longer-legged bronc riders ride with their saddles farther back on horses than shorter-legged guys.

I use a helper to saddle a horse because I think it's the safest and most efficient way to do it. I handle everything up top, above the chute from the back side of the chute, and he works down below, on the other side of the chute. I

Getting ready to get on my 10th bronc at the 1998 NFR. He's tied in because he likes to flip in the chute. (Shari Van Alsburg photo)

don't send my helper down below to do my dirty work or because I don't want to take the chance of hurting myself. The things we both do are safe as long as we do them right. It's just that I can't be both places at the same time.

When the saddle's sitting on the horse's back, I drop my helper the latigo. He grabs it and puts it through the cinch ring. Then I reach down and pull it up on my side. At that point, I pull my cinch only tight enough to keep the saddle snug and in place if the horse jumps around in the chute.

When the front cinch is set, my helper hooks the back cinch by the buckle with a hook and pulls it toward him. Then I reach down and grab the buckle, and buckle it from the top side. I leave the back cinch hanging down three inches below the horse's belly until right before I ride. I don't want it looser than that because I don't want to risk the horse hanging a leg in it if he kicks in the chute, and I don't need it tighter.

Once my saddle's set, I judge the horse again. If he's doing fine, I leave him alone. If he's still nervous, I pet him some more. I realize at times like that how fortunate I was to ride all those racehorse colts with my dad when I was a kid. It wasn't always fun going out there in the cold at 4 o'clock in the morning. But now I look back and realize how important it was for me to learn so much about horses.

I start pulling my front cinch tight when there are four horses to buck ahead of mine. If I'm one of the first few guys to ride, I listen to the chute boss and go from there.

I tighten the cinch slowly and gently. If a horse is cinchy and wants to hold his breath and blow up, I hold the end of the latigo, and keep steady pressure on it without pulling tighter. When the horse exhales, I ease it a little tighter. Jerking on the cinch and trying to take too much at one time is a mistake. A horse can hold his breath for that short a time, so that's a good way to end up nodding with a loose saddle.

To make sure my cinch is as tight as it needs to be, I grab the gullet of my saddle and lift straight up. I want my cinch tight enough so it doesn't move at all off the horse's back when I lift on it. Once I get a bronc pulled, which takes about three minutes, I tie off the cinch by taking the latigo and looping it over and around the front of the d-ring and back between the top and second layers of latigo. Then I pull the tail of the latigo from each side back flat under the back of the saddle and cross them. It's the flattest, flushest way to tie the latigos off so they won't interfere with my legs.

When the guy ahead of me leaves the chute, I pull the back cinch with a slow, steady motion, keeping it angled to the back end of the horse so it runs just behind the break of the belly and won't be in the way of my feet when I'm trying to spur. That angle also keeps the saddle from riding forward. I pull the back cinch tight enough so the back of the saddle won't come up when the horse bucks; so it can serve its purpose of keeping the saddle down in constant contact with the horse, and from going over his head.

When I'm up, I measure my rein *one* time. Remeasuring it only messes with guys' heads because they start second-guessing themselves. That horse's neck isn't going to grow between the time I measure my rein and the time I nod. I also stand a lot better chance of getting along with a horse if I can get in and out of there without pulling on his head more than I have to.

Once I've gotten my measurement, I hold my rein at the spot I've chosen. I hold it between my thumb and index finger, and between my ring finger and pinky, and at the base of my fingers because it's easier to squeeze that way than if it's across my palm.

With my rein in my hand, I get up on the chute and put my arenaside foot on the saddle to let the horse know I'm coming. Then I sit down in the saddle, keeping my hand down so there's slack in my rein. That way, if the horse jerks his head he won't jerk the rein away from me.

I usually put my right foot in the stirrup first because it's opposite my left hand, which I use to reach down and get my stirrups (because my right hand's on the rein). When I'm reaching down with my left hand to get my stirrups, I brace my right arm on top of the chute so that while I'm bent down I have a sense of safety if the horse rears up or jumps around. I always get the easiest stirrup first, which usually ends up being the right one. But if a horse is leaning to the right, for example, I get the left one first. If a horse is calm and still in there, I get both stirrups at the same time.

After both my feet are in the stirrups, I put my legs against the swells of the saddle, with my feet drawn back to the cinch. My body position is back so my feet are "light," which means I can easily place them where they need to be when the horse leaves the chute — at the point of the break of the shoulder on each side. That body position gives me a wider and easier range of motion with my feet.

I don't pull myself forward in the saddle before I nod, like some guys do, because if I did that I'd slide back when the horse blew out of there. I just sit where it's comfortable when my legs and arms are in their proper positions — with my free arm resting on top of the chute (or gate, depending on the delivery) until the horse commits himself, just like in the bareback riding.

Finally, I take the slack out of my rein by moving my hand up and out in front of me, so I won't spur over it. I don't jerk the rein up in the air because that might make a horse flip. I don't want slack in the rein when I nod, either, or I'll slide back in the saddle until I hit the end of the rein. When both hands and feet are where I want them, and I have a comfortable seat in the saddle, I nod.

I wait for a horse to commit himself before I reach forward with my feet and set them in front of the neck for the spur-out. I don't set my feet when he's just standing there, just like in the bareback riding, because he's more likely to be startled by that and come over backwards. When a horse is rearing out of there, it's harder to get my feet set because I'm working against his momentum when he's jumping away from me. So I reach to set my feet as he's peaking and breaking over; when the momentum's back in my favor. It's a lot easier, and it still gives me time to get my feet set before the horse's front feet hit the ground that first jump out of the chute.

I like to spur a bronc out two jumps for the same reasons as in the bareback riding; basically because I think it helps set up a good ride. From there, I'm in the groove and can go right on with a horse and get in time with him.

The spur-out is the only time my body's back while the horse is moving forward in the bronc riding. My feet are set and my legs are in his neck, which helps carry me with the horse. Lifting on my rein as the horse is leaving the chute also helps the horse carry me back down with him after each jump.

I start to spur a bronc on the third jump, as the horse starts to leap into the air. I bring my body forward to counteract the jump, so my momentum is going in the same direction as the horse's. At the same time, my feet start to go back toward the cantle.

A full spur stroke starts in front of the horse's shoulders and goes to the back of the cantle each jump. My toes are turned out and my knees stay right up against the swells of the saddle the whole way. Keeping my legs against the swells and squeezing the swells with my knees helps me hold on and stay in control of the ride.

As the horse peaks, my feet are at the cantle. As he breaks over, I start to go back to the front with my feet. Leaning back helps me set my feet, and setting my feet helps keep my body position back where it needs to be. The combination keeps me square, and from getting whipped forward.

This horse flipped on me in the ninth go at the 1990 NFR. The swell of the saddle hit my knee, which took me out of the 10th round. (PRCA photo)

Spurring a bronc at La Fiesta de los Vaqueros in Tucson during my rookie year in the PRCA, 1988. (James Fain photo)

Winning the Ellensburg Rodeo on Flying 5 Rodeo's 1999 PRCA Bucking Horse of the Year Spring Fling. (Dan Hubbell photo courtesy of Buckers, Inc.)

"Drag" is the spur contact I keep with a horse throughout a ride. The amount of drag I want depends on the horse. That contact's not nearly as important on a quick, rapid-fire kind of horse as it is on a stronger horse. On a quick horse there isn't as much time to get a lot of drag, and I don't need as much of it to stay on. On a more powerful horse, drag keeps me in contact with the horse while he's jumping away from me, so I don't get left behind. It's harder to turn loose with my spurs and then get them reset on a horse like that, with that much momentum going away from me.

It is possible to make a bucking horse look a little harder than he really is to ride, and sometimes get a few extra points by overexaggerating the countermoves. It's not easy to do, so it's probably worth the extra points on the cowboy's side of the score. Because of the degree of difficulty it takes to do that, it's usually only done at the professional level.

The most important thing on the spur ride in both bucking horse events is to stay ahead of the horse with my feet. The judges want to see my feet set before the horse's front feet hit the ground; not as they hit the ground.

My free arm works as a pilot in the bronc riding, just like it does in the bareback riding. When my body needs to go forward (as the horse jumps), I move my free arm forward and then follow it with my body. When my body needs to go back (when the horse kicks), I move my free arm back, and that pulls my body back with it.

This one's throwing a wild horse fit in Clovis, California in 1991. When a horse does that it's tough — it feels like it's all uphill. (Fred Nyulassy photo)

Getting off safely at the whistle is really important in every event because it can be the difference between riding tomorrow and turning out.

When the whistle blows, I usually just keep riding with one hand unless the horse is running off or lurching ahead. I keep using my free arm for balance, spurring only as much as I need to to keep in time with the horse. When I do double-grab after the whistle, it's on the rein. I use both hands for more power to try to bring the horse's nose around and slow him down.

In the saddle bronc riding, I don't hand my rein over to the pickup man until I either have my other hand on him or am committed to making my move to the back of his horse. I wait because if I hand my rein over before I'm ready to get off and the pickup man drops it, I'm in trouble. Sitting in the saddle with the rein dangling between a horse's front legs while he's running off is dangerous because he could step on the rein and fall or go end-over-end. It's also really hard to keep my balance with nothing in my hand.

It's important to kick my feet out of both stirrups at the same time, but I don't do it until I've committed my whole body to getting off. Otherwise, I'll be on top of that horse with no stirrups. If things widen between me and the pickup man, and I can't get off, I'll be hung out to dry.

Jumping off a bronc at the "Daddy of 'em All" in Cheyenne after a winning ride. (Jan Spencer photo)

Using the bronc's momentum to get over to the pickup horse. (Cowpix photo)

Just as in the bareback riding, it's a lot easier to get off on the pickup man if a bronc is still bucking, not running off. That buck gives me the momentum I need to send me over to the pickup horse.

Once I'm on the pickup horse, I wait for the pickup man to slow down, turn away from the bronc and let me down. If the pickup man's dallied my rein to his saddle horn, it's especially important that I get off on the side of the pickup horse away from the bronc. I keep my feet up on the pickup horse's butt until I think it's safe to get off. I don't ever want to hang between the two horses because that exposes me to getting kicked.

Because I only go to the biggest and best PRCA rodeos, I have the advantage of the best pickup men in the world. At other rodeos, where the pickup men aren't as experienced,

it's even more important to do your part and not rely on them, because your safety's on the line.

If I'm getting bucked off in the saddle bronc riding, I want to be belly-down with my toes down so my feet can come out of the stirrups. It's dangerous to be belly-up because the stirrups are locked on my feet. It's a good idea to try to get belly-down when getting bucked off in any event so I don't expose my face and all my vital organs to getting kicked or stepped on. Also, I'm ready when I hit the ground to get up and out of there. It's also easier to tumble and roll if I'm face-down. Of course, I always try to land on my feet, because it doesn't hurt as bad and I'm ready to run as soon as I hit the ground.

My dad makes my bronc reins, and they're half poly and half grass. I like how grass feels because it isn't slippery. But an all-grass rein gets too affected by the weather; too stiff when it's cold and too soft when it's hot. The poly gives me the texture and longevity I like. It also gives a rein strength for when the pickup man dallies up with a stout bronc on the end of it.

The first foot of my rein, the part that connects to the halter, is small, all poly and tightly braided so if I spur over my rein my spur won't get stuck in it. A four-strand braid is used the full length of my rein, but each strand ranges from four to 16 pieces of twine. So there are 16 pieces of twine at the small end and 64 at the thick end. My rein

starts small, and where I hold it it's thick and loosely braided. The length of my rein is the length of the span of my outstretched arms (fingertip to fingertip), about six feet long.

Stock contractors provide the bronc halters at most professional rodeos. There are a row of them hanging on a fence when you get back behind the chutes. I have one, which I've used for practice, that I carry with me. I think it's a good idea to carry one, especially when you're starting out, because you can't always bank on one being provided for you.

The seat of a saddle fits properly if you can sit in it and put three or four fingers between the front of the swell and the inside center of your knee. I rode the bronc saddle Jim

Sitting in my bronc saddle, getting my rosin right. (Cowpix photo)

Sharp used in college, a G Bar G (Sheridan, Wyoming) the first 10 years of my professional career (through the 1998 NFR). Now I ride a Dave Dahl saddle (Fort Pierre, South Dakota). Both saddles have 16 ¼-inch seats in them.

There are a few ways to adjust a bronc saddle to fit you just right. The quarter-bind straps are located under the seat,

a tiny amount, but that's what quarter binds are for; and that's why blocks aren't necessary, in my opinion.

Front binds are adjustments that keep the stirrup pressure consistent throughout a spur stroke. Without them you'd have to spur with a straight leg to keep the slack out of the stirrup leather. Front binds act as a knee joint for the stirrup

My old bronc saddle with the seat lifted up so you can see some of the binds. (Kendra Santos photo)

beneath the seat cover that flaps open. The quarter binds are screwed into the tree of the saddle, and are there to make half an adjustment. They compensate for the stirrup-leather holes that make three-quarter-inch adjustments. If the big buckle on the stirrup leather doesn't get the stirrup just the right length, the quarter-bind adjustment splits the difference. Basically, quarter binds are used for fine-tuning.

Some guys use what they call blocks, which are pieces of leather with buckle holes in them that go under the big buckle on the stirrup-leather adjustment. Blocks are as wide as the stirrup leathers, and are 2 1/2 inches long. The two buckle tongues, held in place by the stirrup-leather buckles, secure the blocks in place. Blocks shorten the stirrup length

leather because the leg doesn't stay straight throughout the spur stroke. When your leg's extended, you need the whole stirrup length. But when it's bent back to spur to the cantle you only need half the stirrup-leather length. When you tighten your front bind, it shortens the amount of stirrup it lets you have when you're spurring back to the cantle.

I use the same kind of extra-wide front cinch — mine's 9 inches wide — on my bronc saddle as I do on my bareback riggin'. But I use leather latigos on my bronc saddle instead of nylon because I don't have to pull a bronc saddle as tight as I do a bareback riggin' to keep it in place. And I don't tie it off as solidly on the bronc saddle, because leather doesn't slip like nylon does. By using leather I can

60

keep the latigos flatter, so there's less bulk and less of a knot to hit my leg on when I'm spurring. For my back bronc cinch I use a standard leather cinch. On my back billets I have a layer of nylon sewn in between the leather layers for added strength.

The stirrups on my bronc saddle are wood with a metal band around the outside. The plastic stirrups some companies sell break all the time. Even if the wood breaks on my stirrups, the metal will keep it in place to get me through the ride. I wrap tape around my stirrups because it helps hold the wood in place and reduces the slickness of the surface of the stirrup.

My saddle bronc riding spurs. (Kendra Santos photo)

The spurs I use in the bronc riding have an inch-and-a-half-long shank with a three-quarter-inch drop. The drop is there for the same reason as in the bareback riding — so the spur doesn't point at the horse. My bronc spurs, also made by Sam Jenkins, have a dull, five-point rowel on them.

I use a leather heel strap in the bronc riding because bronc riding spurs fit really loose anyway. You want your spurs to move sideways, and up and down in the bronc riding because you're running your spurs alongside the horse. A tight spur can hang up on the cinches; the give of looser-fitting spurs helps them glide over the cinches.

I don't use a glove in the saddle bronc riding because I don't need one; it wouldn't be an improvement. I don't think I could hold a rein as good with a glove. I think it'd actually be harder to hold than with my bare hands. And I don't need any protection when I'm holding a bronc rein because it's loose and long, and doesn't burn my hand.

There are two reasons I don't tie my boots on with a leather strap in the bronc riding like I do in the other events. For one, I won't spur them off with a bronc riding spur stroke. And if I ever hang a foot in a stirrup, I want that boot to come off.

Shin and ankle guards are especially important in the saddle bronc riding, because my ankles hit the cantle, and the buckles on the stirrup leathers will make my shins sore without them.

61

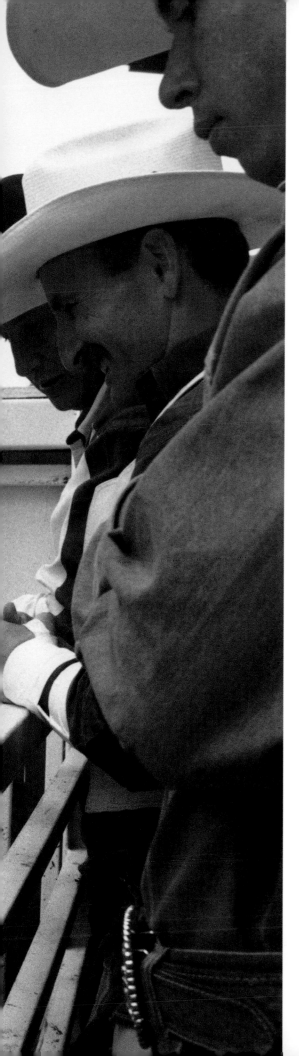

BULL RIDING

The mechanics of bull riding are fairly simple. It's executing them that's hard. Riding bulls is tough physically; it's scary, your adrenaline's pumping, and everything's happening so fast. Bulls are so massive, powerful and smart that making the whistle is a feat in itself.

Because of the degree of difficulty involved, I know that if I go to just 60 rodeos a year and ride every bull I get on at those rodeos and at the NFR I'll be the world champ. That's true for anyone. But it can't be said about the bucking horse events, where it's not so much a question of if I ride, but how well I ride.

Bulls pay attention to what I'm doing to try to ride them. The great ones are masters at feeling where I am, and doing whatever it takes to buck me off. Even if they have a pattern, they'll change it up and try something else if it isn't working. They're smart like horses, but a lot meaner. Nine times out of 10, when a horse acts up in the chute it's because he's scared or nervous. Bulls do it because they're mad — it's that testosterone talking.

After the bronc riding, I take off my bronc spurs and loosen my chaps or take them off, depending on how much time I have between events. Then, before rosining my bull rope, I brush off the old rosin with a wire brush. I brush it just enough to get the old rosin off, so my rope won't get glazed over and slick. I'm careful not to overbrush it, so I don't fray it and wear it out.

To apply rosin in the bull riding, I put rocks of it in my glove and rub it on the top and bottom of the handle and on the part of the tail that I hold. I'm careful not to get any rosin on the wear strip of my rope for two

< Taking my wrap on a bull at the 1999 Cheyenne Frontier Days Rodeo.
(Shari Van Alsburg photo)

reasons: 1.) Because that would make it hard to slide through the loop; and 2.) Because I don't hold on to the wear strip. I hold on to the tail, and hold it in the same place every time. And I adjust my rope to fit each bull by adjusting the loop; not the tail.

After I rosin my bull rope, I put my bull riding spurs on. Then I tape my hand and wrist. I use tape in the bull riding for support because I get sore if I don't. I also do it to prevent jerking callouses off that build up across the base of my fingers if I don't tape my hand. It's painful when that happens, and it takes forever to heal. In fact, there's nothing much more painful than having a big callous ripped off your riding hand. So it sounds funny, but I want to protect my callouses.

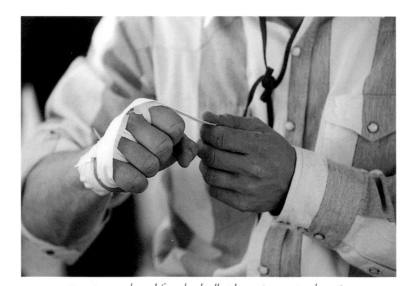

Taping my hand for the bull riding. (Cowpix photo)

I learned a trick when I was a kid in gymnastics that helps manage callouses, which are inevitable as much as I ride. When I'm in the shower, I take a disposable razor and shave them off to smooth them out. I keep them under control by just taking off one thin layer at a time.

As soon as I tape my hand, I put on my chaps and vest, put my glove in my back pocket and tie the leather thong I use to tie on my glove around my neck. Then I climb up on the chute and put my foot on the bull's back so he knows I'm up there and his attention's on me.

I then sit on the bull with my feet on the side slats, my toes pointing straight ahead and spurs straight back. If my feet are turned sideways it's really dangerous because it's easy for them to get caught, twisted and smashed. And if my toes are sticking out the slats, my spurs are into the bull, which can startle him or make him mad. If he jumps forward and runs my feet into one of the bars that run perpendicular to the ground, the chances of tearing up a knee or ankle are excellent. A bull can lean on me when my feet are headed forward, and there's some give because it's flesh on flesh. Another advantage to having my feet on the slats is that I can use my legs to move a bull over in there if he leans on me.

I keep my knees slightly bent when I'm down in the chute so I can stand up and get clear if the bull rears. From that position, I can stand up and brace myself if he kicks and tries to throw me forward in the chute.

Once I'm sitting on the bull, I drop the loop of my rope down the left side of the bull and have a helper reach under the right side with a thick-gauge-wire hook. He grabs the loop with the hook and pulls it far enough under the bull's belly that we can see the rope isn't twisted. I then grab it, and pull the tail of the rope through the loop, bring the handle back to the top side and tie my rope off to the block to keep it in place. I put my bells on the front side of the loop with a simple buckle and strap. My theory on putting them on the front side is that I think it may help keep my rope from sliding backwards, and I use two bells instead of one because that extra weight helps get my rope off of that bull faster than one.

After my rope's set, I get off the bull and go back behind the chutes and stretch my groins and everything else — my hips, neck, torso and arms. I visit with my

Behind the chutes at the 1998 NFR— waiting for the bull riding to start. (Shari Van Alsburg photo)

65

friends some more to stay relaxed, and keep stretching to stay warmed up.

When there are two guys left to ride ahead of me, I put my glove on and use the leather thong from around my neck to tie it on at my wrist. When the bull ahead of mine leaves the chute, I put my foot on the bull's back so he knows I'm coming again. Then I sit on him, with my feet pointed straight ahead and in the slats, and my legs bent slightly at the knee.

At that point, I hand the tail of my rope to the guy pulling it so I can use both hands to position my rope. To do that, I get a little slack in my rope and put it right behind the bull's shoulder blades on top and right behind his front legs on the bottom.

Then I ask my helper for slack, and make sure my bells are directly beneath the bull and centered between his front legs. It's important to make sure the bells aren't pulled up around the side of the bull where my feet will be so they won't interfere with them.

When my rope and bells are where I want them, I ask my helper to pull up on the tail of the rope. That takes the slack out of the rope while I take my gloved hand and run it up and down the tail with rosin to smear it, heat it up and get it tacky. The bottom side of the rope gets heat from my hand, and I get the top side with my thumb.

Then I ask for slack again, and heat the rosin on my handle with four to six strokes. Some guys heat up their ropes for five minutes. In my opinion, that's a waste of time because there's no extra benefit to doing it that long. And since the longer I'm in that chute the better my chances are of getting hurt, I want out of there as fast as possible.

I position my handle so my pinky runs directly down the bull's backbone, right behind his shoulder blades. I then put my hand in the handle and ask my helper to pull my rope. I don't want him to pull it slow or fast; just steady.

I ride with an especially tight rope, so I also use a second helper to pull my rope. I have one guy pull it until it stays put when I pull back on it, then a second helper gets the last little bit. One helper can't usually get my rope tight enough for me. How tight the rope is pulled and how many assistants it takes to do it comes down to personal preference. Harry Tompkins pulled his rope himself. Tuff (Hedeman) used two or three guys. I try to do as much of everything in the chute as I can myself because I want to take charge in there and be in control. I also don't want to have to wait on anybody.

If I have a bull (or horse) that jumps around in the chute and is known to be bad in there, I have one of my helpers "spot" me. The spotter puts one hand in the back of my belt and one hand in front of my chest, so if the bull rears up he has me and can pull me out of there. I use a spotter in the roughstock events for the same reason I used

one in gymnastics — safety — because when I have both hands down, while I'm pulling my rope, I'm vulnerable.

After I've got my rope as tight as I want it, I get my wrap by twisting the rope half a turn so the cupped side lays flush over the lace on my handle. Then I close my hand and take a full wrap around the back of it with the tail of my rope. The rope comes over the top of itself and lays in front of the two plies (the handle on bottom and tail on top), on edge.

Once I get my wrap, I take the tail of my rope and set it on top of the bull's shoulders so I can grab it with my free hand when the whistle blows and loosen my wrap so my riding hand will come free when I get off. I then scoot all the way up to my hand, with my feet still in the slats, and sit down on the bull. I take my feet out of the slats and move them down by my rope, turn my toes out and nod.

I want to be sitting up straight when I nod, with my free hand on the gate or back of the chute, depending on the delivery, in the ready position but not tense. I take my hand off the gate or chute (depending on the delivery) when it starts to open, and put my free arm wherever it needs to be to get a 90-degree angle at the elbow.

I call for a bull in a neutral position, sitting straight up, because bulls have 100 different ways of leaving the chute. When a bull commits himself out the gate, nine times out of 10 I lean forward to move with him, because nine times out of 10 it's a forward motion he's leaving there with. Sitting in the middle and lifting on my rope keeps me square and balanced, and allows me to move with the bull. If I'm already leaning forward and a bull jumps out of there, I have nowhere to go but back.

A lot of guys "jump" at bulls. By that I mean they nod sitting back off of their ropes, then jump up onto their ropes when the gate opens. Larry Mahan used to do that a

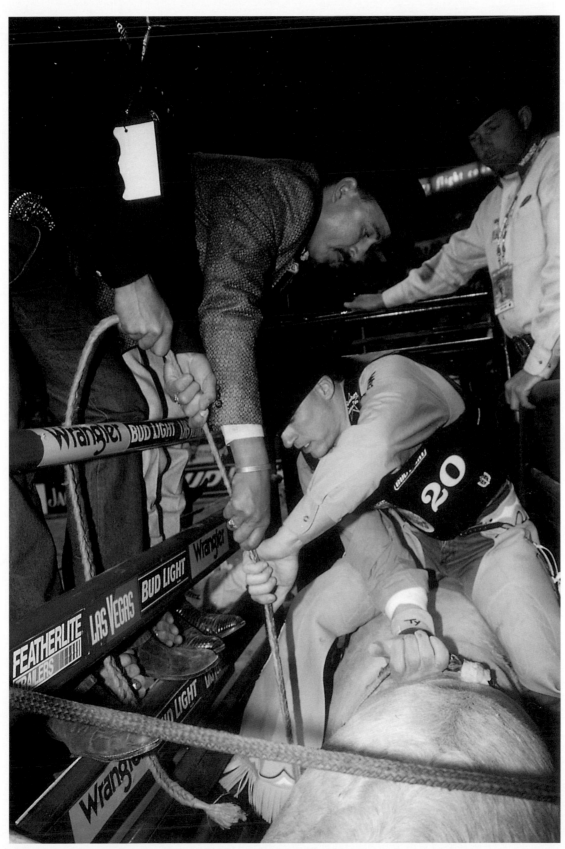

Pulling my rope on Don Kish's Vindicator in the third round of the 1999
PBR Finals. I won the round with 90.5 points. (Shari Van Alsburg Photo)

lot, because he felt like it got him up and moving, and off of his butt. In my opinion, doing that leaves too much room for error and playing catch-up.

I nod with my spurs touching the bull, but with no pressure. I don't take my first "holt" with my feet (set them and get ahold of the bull with my spurs) until the bull commits himself out the gate, because I don't want to stick him in the chute and cause him to fight it.

To be successful, I need a counter move for every move a bull makes, and I need to make my moves at the same time the bull makes his for it to work. That's bull riding simplified.

I also have to keep my weight on my crotch and legs. When a bull's going right, I need to shift my weight to my right leg to keep from getting bucked off to the left, and shift it while I'm leaning forward to counter the bull's lunge. Every time a bull jumps, my body has to move forward with him. When a bull's kicking, the counter move is having my body leaned back. When a bull's flat, I need to be sitting straight up. When I'm sitting straight up and down I'm neutral because I can move wherever I need to to counter his next move.

Bull riding is all about beating the obstacle when it arises. Bulls are so strong, and they're always trying to get away from you. After years of riding you just get a feel for bulls; a good idea of what they're going to do before they do it. I can sometimes tell a bull's going to change directions before he does it. But that's something everyone has to feel and learn for himself, because there's no way to explain that feeling.

Moving out of the chute with a bull. (Shari Van Alsburg photo)

Buddy Pinz's Mega Bucks is spinning right, into my riding hand. I let my free arm swing up over my head to the right to shift my weight, and let loose with my left foot to spur him. (Dan Hubbell Photo)

Riding Terry Williams' Red Wolf in round two at the 1999 PBR Finals for 95.5 points. I won third. That was one of the toughest rounds in bull riding history. (Watson Rodeo Photos)

I don't want to ride with a hump in my back because it'll scoot me back on my butt, and sitting on my butt will make my riding arm straight. When I'm up on my crotch and leaning forward, my riding arm is bent, like it needs to be. That way, when a bull peaks and breaks over, I have a shock absorber for that jerk and won't get tilted over to my riding-arm side as much.

It's important to sit on my crotch and not my butt in the bull riding, because I want the weight of my body running down my legs; not on my butt. I talked about positioning my body so my feet are light in the horse events, but in the bull riding I want my legs down and heavy. Sitting on my butt makes my feet light, which just gets me jerked down because I can't get a holt with them.

The hardest place to recover from in the bull riding is when I get tilted into my riding hand. When I get tilted to the right, I have to try to get weight back on my left leg using my free arm so I can get centered again. Lane Frost taught me to keep trying to keep my weight going down both legs. I get that by staying up on my crotch, which makes it easier to keep my feet in a bull and move forward with him.

Most guys like bulls that buck "into their hands," the same direction as their riding hands. If they're right-handed, for example, it's easier to pull themselves back to center from being off to the left than it is if they're tilted off to the right. Since I ride right-handed, when I'm falling over to the left side my right foot is naturally coming up the side

This bull got me jerked back to the end of my riding arm. He jerked me into my riding hand so hard that he almost threw me out in front of him. (PRCA photos by Dan Hubbell)

A famous bull of Dan Russell's called White Lightning at the 1992 NFR. He's spinning to the left and trying to well me in the middle photo. In the third photo, I'm getting ready to cut loose and try to get a new holt with my right foot. (PRCA photos by Mark Reis courtesy of Buckers, Inc.)

of the bull. That's when I need to get my weight back over to the right. As the bull peaks and breaks over, I have a chance to drop my right foot back down and reset it.

If you want to stand a chance of being a great bull rider, you need to learn to ride them all, no matter which way they go. Because if you can only ride bulls that go one direction, you're only a 50-percent bull rider. I personally don't care which way a bull spins, as long as he does spin.

Spurring is not required in the bull riding, and neither is a spur-out. It's up to the cowboy whether or not he wants to risk taking his feet out of a bull to spur him. Unlike the horse events, I never spur a dink in the bull riding. It's funny, because when I was a kid that's the only kind of bull I spurred. But at the professional level, I don't think spurring a dud does me any good. What's the difference between being 62 or 63 points? Either way, I'm not going to win anything.

I do spur the good ones, even though I think spurring a good bull can sometimes hurt a guy because it can take away from the bull's half of the score. It's better for the cowboy's half of the score to try and make bulls look even better than they are; not the other way around. But if I'm going to spur a bull he's going to be a good one. I like to spur bulls that are outstanding enough that the judges are going to realize that spurring them isn't easy.

When I'm riding as aggressively as I have to to ride a really good bull, the decision of whether or not to spur him is something that becomes instinctive with experience, and is just part of knowing how to win, just like helping a bull look harder to ride than he really is.

It's possible to make a bull look a little better than he really is by overexaggerating the counter moves. If a bull takes a jump forward, for example, I can move forward and bring my free arm even further forward than I really need to. Another way to dress up a bull is to let him start into the spin without me, then make a bigger, more exaggerated move to catch up, and do that again the next jump. Only the best cowboys in the world even recognize things like free-arm fancy work and playing catch-up as hamming it up. It's not cheating, and it's not easy to do. It just looks better, and is another way of showing your talent. Before he retired, Ted Nuce (the 1985 PRCA world champion bull rider) was the master at making bulls look better than they were.

Jim Sharp (who won world bull riding championships in 1988 and '90) can ride bulls so flawlessly that it sometimes hurts him. He can make rank bulls look easy; like they had an off day. When he's riding like that, Jim's in such perfect sync with a bull that it almost looks effortless; like the bull's a lot easier to ride than he really is.

Like most guys, I usually spur bulls with my outside foot because I use my inside foot to hold what I have while the bull's jumping away from me. When the bull breaks over and gives me back some momentum, I take my outside foot out of him just long enough to get another holt. Resetting my foot like that gets me back over to the middle. The reason I usually spur with my outside foot is because I have to keep ahold with my inside foot when a bull is trying to throw me to the outside. I don't spur with my inside foot because that's what I'm holding on with.

Since I'm right-handed, when a bull's spinning to the right he's trying to buck me off to the left. As a bull jumps and I move my body over to the right, I can take my foot out of him and reset it. As the bull moves forward, my left foot is running up his side. As the bull gives some momentum back to me, I pull my foot out and reset it. During all of this, I'm trying to keep my right foot down and to keep a holt with it, because it's all that keeps me from going off the left side, where the bull's momentum's trying to send me.

I've noticed in pictures that you can usually tell by my free hand how things are going with a ride. I don't purposely think about holding my fingers a certain way, but when my hand is open and my ring and middle fingers are together, that's a sign that I'm relaxed and everything's going great. When my free hand is balled up in a fist is when I'm stiff, straining and struggling to stay on.

Keeping my free arm at a 90-degree angle is important in the bull riding, because if it gets too high it'll tilt me off to the side. Keeping it down helps keep me square, and I need to be centered every time the bull hits the ground with his front feet.

No matter what the bull does and what I'm doing to counter it, I finish every move with my free arm out in front. That way, I'm neutral and ready for whatever the next move might be. My free arm can make or break me in the bull riding. If I have control of it and am using it to get where I want to be, it makes me. If the bull has control of it and whips it on me, it breaks me and gets me bucked off.

If a bull's bucking into my hand, it's easier to get back into position because I have more momentum with my free arm. I can throw my free arm straight over my head and pull myself back into position, in the center of the bull's back.

When a bull bucks away from my riding hand (in my case that means he's spinning left and trying to throw me off to the right) it's a helpless feeling, because I'm fighting the air with my free arm and fighting gravity. So when a bull does go away from my hand I have to lean forward when he jumps to counter that forward movement for two reasons: 1.) Because I need to go with the bull to counter his move away from me; and 2.) Because from that position I can get the momentum behind my free arm to move back over to the center and get squared up.

After shifting my weight to the center, with my free arm on the left side, I can reset my left foot — after the peak and before the bull's front feet hit the ground. Until that point, I have no choice but to hold what I have with my left foot because it's all I've got; when a bull's moving away from me is no time to take my foot out of him.

Some bulls are what cowboys call "welly." That means they try to throw you off into the inside of the spin. A welly bull is actually moving out away from me while he's in the air, so he leaves me hung out to dry on the inside of

This bull is turning back to the right. I'm moving my free arm over and in front to be ready for the next jump. (PRCA photo by Dan Hubbell)

This is the kind of bull riding form I shoot for every time. (Dan Hubbell photo)

the well. He doesn't push me to the inside, he just moves out to where he creates that well and drops me down in it. Welly bulls usually buck flat, because they're swinging their butts instead of kicking. Another thing I've noticed about them is that they're usually mean. They try to get you in that well so they can hook you.

I counter welly bulls by countering the jump more than the kick. I move forward as the bull starts to jump; then I'm ready for the next jump. Since there isn't much kick

and his butt's just swinging, doing that keeps me from getting strung out.

When I do get caught in the well, it's dangerous because the bull's bucking around me and it's hard to get out. There is a counter move I use to try to get out. Since I ride right-handed, if a bull spins to the left I reach with my free arm in front of me and to the right to shift my body weight to my right leg. I then hold on with my right foot until I can get my weight shifted after the peak of the jump and can reset my foot.

This bull is kicking really high. My free arm is a little too high and whipped to the right. There's a gap under my left leg, which shows there's no weight on it. Jim Sharp and the late Lane Frost watched this ride from behind a chutegate at La Fiesta de los Vaqueros in Tucson. (James Fain Photo)

The reason bulls like Sammy Andrews' Bodacious, David Bailey's Gunslinger and Playboy were so rank is because they had so much "drop." Just like in the horse events, a bull is considered "droppy" if his front feet are still off the ground when he's kicking, and he has to drop back down to the ground with his front end after he extends and kicks with his back feet.

When a bull drops in front, it naturally jerks my riding arm down. When that happens, my free arm gets whipped back and behind my head, which shifts all my weight to the side of my riding arm. That's what'll get me thrown off that side when a bull drops. With that free arm acting as my pilot, when it goes off to that side, I usually do, too. To stay in control, my free arm has to work for me, and in that case it works against me.

When I'm on a bull, I don't fix my eyes on any one thing and zero in on it. My balance is better when I'm aware of everything that's going on in front of and around me, and keep a perspective of the bull, the ground, the fence and the bull-fighter. I try to keep my head down and my chin tucked, because when my head goes up everything else goes up with it.

—🤠—

Good get-offs are just as important as good rides to anyone interested in a long, successful career, and if you learn to do it the right way, it's easy. I learned to get off of bulls by watching Cody (Lambert). He was so good at it that he could get off a bull going into his hand.

When the whistle blows, I grab my second wrap with my free hand and pull it out of my riding hand while I'm still holding onto the first wrap. When I pull my tail, I slide my left hand up to the end of the tail so I can use that momentum with my free arm to throw me off the right side as I get off.

I wait until the bull's either going straight or bending to the left, because it's important for a right-handed rider like me to get off the right side. There are five basic reasons why I want to get off on the same side as my riding hand: 1.) My rope was designed to allow my hand to come out easier on that side, and if I get off on the other side my riding hand could hang up against the block of the rope. When I go off the right side there's room for my hand to slide down and give me slack in the handle. 2.) Bullfighters are trained to take bulls away from my hand (to the left) after the whistle, so I want to go the other direction. 3.) Since the right side is the side my rope's pulled from, it's the side that loosens when there's slack in the rope. 4.) If I get off on the off-side (the side opposite my riding hand) and my hand's still in the rope, I can't open my hand because it's locked in against the block. 5.) When I get off on the off-side I take all the slack in the rope with me so it won't loosen.

These days, if a bull's still spinning into my hand after I get my wrap I wait for the bullfighters to take the bull straight away or bend him back to the left so I can get off on the right and not have him on top of me. At the professional level it's easier to stick to your game plan, because the bullfighters are better. They know to take a bull away from your riding hand and how to do it.

When I was a junior rodeo, high school and amateur bull rider, I used to get off whichever side looked safest. At that level, the bullfighters aren't always real experienced, so a lot of times it's a save-your-own-butt situation.

Just before I get off, I'm still squeezing my rope in my hand, with my free hand on the tail and my legs in position down by my rope. As the bull starts to jump, I lean my body weight forward and to the right, and then, as the bull peaks and starts to kick, I let that momentum throw me clear. I turn loose with both hands as I commit myself to jump off. I want to hit low and let my knees absorb the shock. Once I do hit, I bend over low so if a bull kicks in my direction he won't kick me in the back or the back of the head.

77

This is Harper and Morgan's Bart Simpson. He bucked in the eliminator pen at the Finals, and was bad to belly roll with you. It looks like I'm so mad at getting bucked off that I want to choke myself. (Dan Hubbell Photo)

I never get off a bull that's standing still. Because if he's flat-footed, it's nothing for him to spin around and hook me. I never get off on the fence, either, even if a bull's standing still right next to it, because I have no idea what's on that fence. I could cut my hand on an old nail or catch my finger on a piece of wire. Worse than that, I could get draped out on the fence and leave myself wide open to getting kicked.

Remember, it isn't over when you get off. You need to keep tending to business until you get to a safe place before you start tipping your hat or winking at your girlfriend. If you can get up, do it and get out of there. You might have a sore foot, but that's better than a sore head, face or whole body. In fact, the way I see it, you better be unconcious or dead before you just lay out there and don't try to get away.

The only time I've ever laid out there in the arena in the bull riding was when I was knocked out. Being tough is not an option in this sport, and there are times when it can save your life. I realize that when you're hurt in the arena the best thing you can do medically is lay still. But realistically, 2,000-pound bulls don't care if you hurt your knee or your shoulder. So the longer you lay there, the greater chance you have of getting killed. Bulls don't care that you twisted your ankle. Nobody does, except maybe your mom.

If I get hung up in the bull riding, it's important to try to stay on my feet. If I'm not on my feet, the back of my legs will get stepped on every time the bull's hind legs hit the ground. Then, when he jerks me loose, I'll end up flat on my face. Also, when all of my weight is hanging from my riding hand, it's about impossible to open it. If I can get up on my feet, I can get up above my rope and get my hand out because I can take the pressure off of my hand.

When a bull falls down with me, the first thing I do is see if my hand's going to come out. If it isn't, I need to ride him out of the fall to give myself more time to get my hand out and make a safe get-off.

When I get back behind the chutes after riding my bull, I stretch some more to prevent being sore the next day. I stretch while I'm putting my equipment away, and keep stretching every chance I get until I go to sleep that night. Stretching after I ride is just as important as before I ride, and it makes a big difference in how I feel the next morning.

—◈—

When you're riding bulls, it isn't over 'til you're out of the arena. Luckily, I got out of this deal alive. (PRCA photo by Dan Hubbell)

Putting a little rosin on my handle at San Jose, California in the early '90s. (Cowpix Photo)

The bull ropes we use today are all poly. The tail of my rope is a five-plait braid; my handle is seven-plait. My dad made my bull ropes until I was 18. These days, Jess Gourley (Carbon, Texas) makes them. I have him put a slight cup in the tail of my rope so it'll lay over the handle and give the rope extra thickness.

If a bull rope's too small, all you'll be squeezing is your own hand. You want your rope to fill your hand when you shut your hand around it.

I like the distance between the top of the handle and the bottom to be about the width of two and a half fingers. With that much slack in it, it tightens down snug after it bends around a bull so my hand's in there solid, but not getting smashed, and I won't hang up after the whistle. If I don't have enough slack, the handle squeezes my hand too hard.

You can order bull ropes in tail and handle combinations of five, seven and nine plaits. I ride with a seven-plait handle and five-plait tail because a seven-plait handle has a tighter braid because more strands are used. By the time the leather is laced into it, it's tight enough to where it won't turn over on me. The five-plait tail I use is softer and easier to squeeze because it has fewer strands in the braid. In general, a hard braid can slip through your hand easier than a softer braid.

Remember, the plait number has nothing to do with the size of your rope. That depends on the size of the rope you start with before you start braiding; on the number and thickness of strands in each braid.

The part of the bull rope made of original, unbraided rope is called the loop. Two adjustable, braided nylon hobbles keep the two round pieces of rope in the loop from twisting.

Two knots are tied on the ends of the two pieces of loop. Those pieces are then braided together with leather. From there, they split off into the top and bottom braid of the handle. The top part has leather laced into it so it won't turn over. Right-handed guys like me ride with the lace running to the right. The leather laces down the middle in a spiral that runs to the right, so when I put my hand in there and lift my hand won't turn over because the spiral will tighten.

Leather is laced into the braided rope to form the block, and there's a riser at the end of the block that keeps my hand from getting pinched and also makes it possible to get my hand out. The riser in my rope is 1 1/4 inches.

After the handle, the rope becomes one again. The "wear strip" is where the rope runs through the loop. When I pull my rope, the wear strip rubs on the loop. I like to sew leather on my wear strip, because that's where a rope wears out first.

Like I said before, I buy the best equipment, take good care of it and stick with it. When I won my first world bull riding championship in 1993, the rope I won it with was three years old. Cody convinced me before the Finals that year that it might break. So I had a piece of leather sewn on the wear strip.

That rope felt so good that I kept riding with it even after the Finals. I was still using it that next July (1994) at Salinas (the California Rodeo). I drew the best bull in the herd there, Sonny Riley's red bull Dog Face. I made a deal with God that day. I swore to him that if he'd get me through that ride with that rope I'd retire it. I won Salinas, and

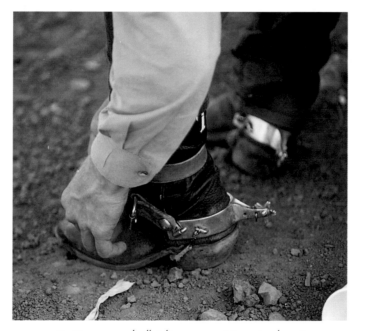

Putting on my bull riding spurs. (Cowpix photo)

cracked out a new rope the next day at Cheyenne (Frontier Days Rodeo in Wyoming).

It was a fad a few years ago to roll up a bull rope before you put it away. Don't do that. When you do, it leaves a curlicue in the end that's dangerous. It can wrap around your leg and break it or grab your spur.

Cody and I designed the pad I use under my bull rope. It's made of high-density foam with a piece of saddle leather sewn on top, which is hard enough to keep my rope from sucking down into the foam. It's covered with a piece of chap leather.

The bottom of the handle can make my index finger sore; from my knuckle rubbing on it. To protect the knuckle on my index finger, I take a thin piece of foam covered with chap leather and sew it to the front of the pad. Then I Velcro it on the back of the pad so it stays put and lays on top of the bottom of the handle. It helps make the bottom of the handle smooth and flat, and protects my hand.

The pad is there to keep me from having to cinch down on a bony back. It keeps my hand from pulling so far down a bull's back, so I don't feel strung out before I leave the chute. That one-inch elevation it gives me makes a big difference. It brings my hand an inch closer to me, and gives me bend in my arm. If I'm strung out with my arm extended in the chute, what am I going to do when a bull jumps in the air, kicks and drops? Before I leave that chute I want to be sitting square with some bend in my elbow.

Jerry Beagley Braiding Company (Calera, Oklahoma) makes my bull riding gloves. They're made of soft deer skin.

I'd rather have my glove a little too thick than too thin. The thickness gives a glove sponginess that helps me hold on to my rope. If a glove's too thin it lacks that sponginess, and gets glazed over with rosin. Unlike some other pieces of equipment, a glove feels the very best the first time you use it.

I tie my bull riding glove on with a thin piece of latigo leather. Tape works, too. The reason I tie it on is so it won't roll down and ball up on me. I don't use any palm pieces in my bull riding glove, because they aren't necessary.

I use black rock rosin on my glove and rope in the bull riding. I hold the rocks of rosin in my hand and then run them down my rope, breaking the rocks under the handle. I make one pass over each side of the handle and over each side of the tail that

Waiting to ride at the Cow Palace in San Francisco. (Cowpix photo)

comes in contact with my hand when I take my wrap. If you do it more than that, you'll just be wearing out your rope for no additional benefit. The heat from the friction makes the rosin sticky, which is what you want in this event as opposed to the others.

All you're trying to do with rosin in the bull riding is smear it in so it collects in the cracks of the braids. You don't want to heat it until right before you ride. That way, it's hot and tacky when you take your wrap.

I use two bells on my rope under a bull's belly. I like the extra weight to pull my rope off after my hand releases, and I think the noise under the bull helps him buck higher. I figure

the commotion of something clanging beneath him has the same effect as a tumbleweed blowing out in front of a colt.

I ride with Kelly 315 spurs (they're no longer made) in the bull riding. They were my dad's. He bought them used for $10 in 1960, back when they were endorsed by Jim Shoulders. When I was 2, we put duct tape around the bands until they were little enough to fit my boots. I've worn them ever since. They're vintage, great spurs, and they're what I'm used to. This is my fourth set of rowels on these spurs, but I don't think the spurs themselves will ever wear out. They're all I've ever ridden with and probably all I ever will ride with.

My bull riding spurs have a two-inch shank and are angled inward 15 degrees. I always try to ride with my toes turned straight out, but if they slip that little angle helps compensate. My bull riding spurs have three-quarters of an inch of drop in the shank, which gives me an extra three-quarters of an inch to reach down and get a holt with my feet.

If you have shorter legs you need shorter-shanked spurs. Longer-legged riders need longer-shanked spurs to close the gap between their feet and the bull. I like brass rowels best. It's a softer metal, and I feel like it gets a holt better. I want my rowels rough but not sharp. Sharp will cut; rough will grab.

I don't want my rowels locked solid because having a little play in them helps keep my feet from bouncing. I put a little piece of coat hanger in the hole on the shank that's right in front of the rowel. It locks them and keeps them from running, but does allow a little play.

If there isn't a hole in the shank of your spurs, get a drill and make one. Drill the hole far enough from the rowel so the prongs on the rowel will hit the wire. You don't want it so close to the pin that it won't go in between the prongs, though. The distance for the hole depends on the size of your rowels.

I tie my boots on in the bull riding with a leather strap designed by my dad. It serves as a combination spur strap and boot strap. Most guys tie their boots on with a long leather thong, which works. I just figure my way is just as effective and removes the need for one more piece of equipment. The strap I use has a buckle on the outside of my foot and a roller buckle with no tongue on the inside of my foot. I take the strap on the outside of my foot, run it over my arch and through the roller buckle, then pull it

The combo straps I use to hold my boots and spurs on in the bull riding. (Kendra Santos photo)

back the other way, go around my ankle and through the buckle. I started using a combination strap when I was 2, because my spur straps were so long that I had to wrap them around my ankle to take out the slack before I could buckle them. It's just something I got comfortable with that made sense even when I grew up.

Mouthpieces are probably a good idea in the roughstock events, though I don't wear one. And I think a helmet would be a great idea if they could design one that wouldn't hinder your vision, and that was light enough that it didn't affect your balance. Your head plays a big part in your balance. It would have to be light enough not to increase your chances of neck injury, and strong enough to really protect you if you got kicked or stepped on.

The bottom line is, any protective equipment that makes you feel better is good as long as it doesn't hinder your ability — that's more dangerous than anything.

KNOWING THE SCORE

One of the first things you need to do if you're serious about riding roughstock is get a PRCA rule book. You have to know the rules before you can play the game. Of course, you can't learn everything you need to know to win just by reading the rule book. Like I've said before, there is no substitute for experience in this sport. At some point, you're going to have to get dirty.

There are some fundamental rules that apply to all three roughstock events, and knowing them is a helpful foundation for anyone who's going to enter or watch; up-and-coming cowboys or fans.

Most PRCA rodeos use two judges, and each judge has a scale of 1-25 points with which to score the cowboy, and another 1-25-point range to mark the horse or bull's performance. So basically, each judge is responsible for a possible 50 points, based half on how hard the animal is to ride and half on how well the cowboy handles the situation and rides him. A 100-point score is possible, and has been done once, by Wade Leslie on Donnie Kish's bull Wolfman at the 1991 PRCA rodeo in Central Point, Oregon. But I don't know that there is such a thing as a "perfect" ride.

Scores in the roughstock events are always going to be an opinion, because it's two human beings judging a ride through their eyes. It's not like the score comes up on a computer screen after the judges punch in some precalculated formula. It's all perception and opinion. Evidently, that 100-point ride was perfect in those judges' eyes on that day. I've seen bulls that bucked harder and guys who rode better, and so have a lot of other guys, but it doesn't matter because they don't write the checks based on the cowboys' opinions. The judges' word is the last word.

< *Behind the chutes at the Cheyenne Frontier Days Rodeo with Cauy Hudson. (Shari Van Alsburg photo)*

Different judges use the points scale differently. One pair of judges will mark a great ride 85 points, and another couple guys might see the same ride as a 95-point ride. It doesn't make much difference as long as they're consistent, and get the placings right. As long as the right guys get the money, it doesn't really matter if they're 90 or 70.

Four judges are used at the National Finals Rodeo, which allows for more opinions and is used to make double sure the best guy wins. With four judges, they add all four scores together, then divide them by two, which also gets rid of a lot of ties.

There are several different ways to get disqualified in each event. In the bareback riding, a cowboy disqualifies himself if: 1.) He bucks off before the eight-second whistle (time starts when the horse breaks the plane of the chute); 2.) He touches the horse, his equipment or another part of his body with his free hand; 3.) He rides with rowels that are either too sharp or locked; 4.) His riggin' comes off the horse, whether it breaks or not; 5.) He fails to spur the horse out of the chute; 6.) He takes a finger tuck or wrap of any kind or uses finger tape; or 7.) He's been advised that he's next to go, and fails to be above the horse with his glove on before the previous horse leaves the arena.

Saddle bronc riding disqualifications include: 1.) Bucking off before the eight-second whistle; 2.) Changing hands on the bronc rein; 3.) Losing or dropping the rein before the whistle; 4.) Wrapping the rein around your hand; 5.) Losing a stirrup; 6.) Touching the horse, equipment or another part of the cowboy's own body with the free hand; 7.) Riding with locked or sharp rowels; 8.) Violating the spur-out rule; 9.) Using any foreign substance besides dry rosin on the chaps or saddle; or 10.) Failing to be above the horse when the previous horse leaves the arena, if advised that you're next to ride.

In the bull riding, a cowboy can be disqualified for any one of six rule infractions. They include: 1.) Bucking off before the eight-second whistle; 2.) Touching the bull, equipment or another part of his body with his free hand; 3.) Using sharp spurs or placing the spurs or chaps under the rope when it's being tightened; 4.) Not having a bell on the bull rope; 5.) Intentionally leaving the chute with your spurs hooked or lodged in the loop(s) of the bull rope; or 6.) Failing to be above the bull with your glove on when the previous bull leaves the arena after being advised that you're next to ride.

The spur-out rule applies only in the bareback and saddle bronc riding, and the basics are the same in both events. To qualify a ride, the cowboy must have his spurs over or above the break of the horse's shoulders and touching the horse (on both sides) when the horse's front feet hit the ground on the initial move out of the chute. The spurs may be rolling on the spur-out in the bareback riding, as long as they're touching the horse when his front feet hit the ground on that initial move out of the chute. "Initial move" can include rearing out, running out, bucking out or stepping out of the chute.

"Free rolls," where a judge yells at a cowboy to "go on," even if the spur-out rule requirements have not been met, may apply when the rider gets fouled in the chute or the horse stalls. If a judge waives the spur-out rule, the cowboy can go on with the ride without spurring the horse out, and receives a score based on the rest of the ride.

Spurring an animal during the ride (after the spur-out) isn't an actual requirement in any event. You won't be disqualified if you don't do it. But failing to spur a bareback horse or bronc, and failing to spur in time with a horse's bucking action, is the kiss of death in the judges' eyes. You won't win a dime if you don't do it.

It isn't always necessary to spur a bull in order to win, and it's definitely the event where spurring is least expected, because it's so hard to have enough control on a bull to do it. Cowboys score in the 90s all the time without spurring bulls, because a great bull's degree of difficulty is so high and staying on him eight seconds without spurring is a feat in itself.

87

With Jim Sharp and Tuff Hedeman at the 1997 St. Louis Open (PBR event).
This was the night I dislocated my right shoulder. (Jennifer Silverberg photo)

A "reride," in which a cowboy gets a second chance on a predesignated bronc or bull, can be awarded to a cowboy by the judges for a number of reasons. If the animal he's attempting to ride runs down the gate and rakes him off, falls, stalls or fouls the cowboy by doing something that keeps him from having a fair competitive opportunity (including not bucking hard enough), the judges may either give that cowboy a score with a reride option or, in the case of an animal falling or stalling, just call for a reride.

There are times in every cowboy's career when he feels like he got burned by the judges; when maybe they might have missed something or said he didn't mark a horse out when he did. When something like that happens to me, I don't ever look at the judges' sheets after the rodeo to see which judge got me. How other people evaluate my rides is beyond my control. I don't want to know which judge to be mad at, because that won't change anything. Getting mad about it is just a waste of time and energy, so I don't bother.

There are other times when fans boo low scores on horses or bulls that leap high into the air. They look wild, but aren't actually as hard to ride as one that has a lot of jump, kick, drop and direction change, and the judges know it. The leapers are usually easier to ride because they aren't going away from you, then breaking over and dropping. They're just going straight up and down, and a lot of times that kind of horse or bull doesn't have any kick.

I compare rodeo judging to Olympic diving, where you're judged on how well you dive *and* the dive's degree of difficulty. I don't think the roughstock events should be

My feet are in the right position here, but I'm not lifting on my rein very well. (PRCA photo)

judged separately, either — with half the score for the cowboy and half for the animal. I don't think you can mark a guy a perfect 25 points on an easy horse or bull, because the degree of difficulty isn't there. I think a cowboy's form should be judged on how hard each animal is to ride, because I don't think those two things can be separated. I don't think a guy should be docked points for not having flawless form on a rank horse or bull, either. Making a good ride on an average animal isn't that big a deal. Making a pretty good ride on a rank animal is a really big deal.

Judges look for a few key elements in each event. In the bareback riding, they consider how much a contestant rolls his spurs toward his riggin', and like to see a rider's toes turned out. Actually, they like to see cowboys' toes turned out in all three events. They look for good timing, and a long spur stroke that runs right up the neck to the riggin'.

According to the PRCA Judges' Handbook, "A perfect (bareback) ride would find the contestant positioning his

Winning the PBR event in Kansas City on Terry Williams' PBR Bull of the Year Baby Face. (Jeff Belden photo)

90

feet high in the neck and rolling his spurs upward toward the riggin'. The length of the stroke, drag, exposure and positioning of the spurs should be considered for marking the ride. For exposure, spurs should be away from the horse when repositioning the feet for the next jump. A rider that rolls his feet up to the riggin' and doesn't throw them out when repositioning his feet would be making just a fair ride, the same as one that rolls them only half the way to the riggin' and throws them out when repositioning. If a rider's feet come back to the flat of the shoulder instead of the neck, he should be marked lower. High markings are awarded to aggressive rides with control and exposure. Things a rider should be penalized for are going to the cinch, getting on tilt and failing to spur."

The PRCA Judges' Handbook encourages judges to look for "aggressiveness, control, timing and length of spur stroke" when evaluating saddle bronc rides. "Timing is a must when a horse changes direction, hesitates, rears, jumps and kicks, or a combination of these things occurs. The length of the stroke should be from high in the neck above the break of the shoulders to the saddle skirts. The rider must be aggressive, and expose himself more to reach the top of the neck (by extending his spur stroke). To achieve a high marking, a contestant must have his toes turned out, with his spurs touching the animal, and use a full stroke without stopping; set his feet; follow with a

Spurring Mack Altizer's Tequila for 87.5 points in the first round at the 1999 PBR Finals. (Watson Rodeo Photos)

good drag; and maintain control for the entire length of the ride. Points are lost if the rider is not balanced and in control (if he gets tilted off to one side), and are gained or lost according to the rider's rhythm and timing with the horse's bucking."

The advice given judges in the bull riding event by the PRCA Judges' Handbook includes, "Adding points for good body position and movements; use of free arm or shoulders; and spurring to adjust for the bull's bucking style and to help maintain control. Spurring a bull in the neck is worth more points than spurring behind the shoulder. Staying in the middle of the bull in full control of the ride, without being on tilt or reared back, is what is desired and should be scored accordingly. Points should be deducted for a contestant who cannot maintain control; gets on tilt; or does not stay in the middle of the bull. Winning rides should be on the rank animals when the contestant shows aggressiveness and control."

Generally, the "nice" broncs and bulls have a lot of jump and kick, but not a lot of drop, where their front ends drop so far so fast that it feels like their heads disappear. And each jump is usually a lot like the one before it, which makes it possible for the cowboy to get in time with the animal. If you watch the riggin' in the bareback riding, for example, it won't be moving much throughout the ride. On a nice horse or bull, the cowboy has a good seat the whole way, and has

91

so much control that he's trying to see how perfect he can make it look.

The "rank" ones, that are the hardest to ride and are worth the most points, have a lot of jump, kick, drop and direction changes. On some of the best rides, the cowboy never knows from one jump to the next if he's going to be there. He's always loose and scrambling, and trying to get that good seat. The rank bucking horses and bulls are so smart that they'll change what they're doing to try to buck you off if it isn't working, and try something else.

The nice ones and the rank ones are both good, as long as they buck the whole eight seconds, because if you do your part you can win on them. Personally, I'd rather have a rank one, because I have a chance to earn more points by making a great ride on a horse or bull of that caliber. It's harder to do my job on a rank one, but I like that challenge. When a horse or bull really bucks, I know he's going to get a lot of points. And if I do my job right, so will I.

To compare riding roughstock to diving again, the nice ones are like swan dives, and the rank ones are like triple-twisting backflips. I go at both kinds of animals the same way, and try to stick to the basics and do everything right no matter what I draw because that works on every kind of horse or bull. From there, I have to compensate for each jump, depending on what the animal's doing.

The nice horse or bull, like the swan dive, might be worth 17 or 18 points based on the degree of difficulty, and I might get 22 points on my form if I do everything perfectly, which I know I can. If everything goes right, a ride or dive of that degree of difficulty is worth about 80 points.

The rank animal, or triple-twisting backflip, is worth 23 points on each side, or potentially about 92 points if everything goes right. Of course, there's a greater chance I'll mess up and not win anything. But that's a chance any good cowboy is willing to take. I'd try the triple-twisting backflip every time, because getting things done right under the gun is my job.

The bottom line to all of this, as cowboys, is that we don't get to pick what we get on. I've got to be ready to make my best possible ride no matter which animal I've drawn. Even if I draw a dud, I have to do my job the very best I can do it. That way, I stay sharp and am ready to get it done when I do get a good one.

In my opinion, the most important trait in a judge is a really experienced eye; one that gives him the ability to judge the horse or bull separately from the cowboy. When watching a ride, you have to be able to see how hard a bull's *really* bucking, not based on how hard the guy makes it *seem* like he's bucking; regardless of whether the guy's making it look easy or having hell. The animal's half of the score is his alone, and should not be affected by what the cowboy does. The cowboy's half of the score, on the other hand, depends on the degree of difficulty thrown at him by the animal.

Like I said in the bull riding chapter, Jim Sharp sometimes makes bulls look so easy that he even fools me into thinking they aren't bucking very hard. I've seen a bull he rode marked 21 points, and I was fooled right along with the judges into thinking he didn't look that bad. Then, a week later, that bull might stick my head in the ground and was marked 24 points when I had him.

A good judge has to be able to tell the difference between an animal that's truly rank or easy, and one that just looks that way depending on who's riding him. He has to be able to tell how rank an animal is simply by how rank he is and nothing else. It's frustrating to see a guy who's hanging off to the side making big, exaggerated recovery moves that he's only able to make because the bull isn't really rank beat a guy who's right in the middle of a bad son of a gun. The way I see it, making it look easy is my job. I hate to see guys get docked for making it look easy and using perfect form. But that's one of the risks of basing a judging system on human opinions.

I also believe that to be a good judge you have to have competed in each particular event, and have to have been good at it. If you're going to judge world-class rodeo competition, you have to have been there to understand what each guy's up against and what he's having to overcome on each ride. That experienced eye is not something that can be taught; you have to have been there.

Even if it was possible to have only current and former champions judge, every score is still a human opinion. And that's something about rodeo that you might as well get used to, because that's the way it is. Stick to your business, do your best and let the rest go. If you're always worried about the judging, you're fighting your head. And that's no way to rodeo — or live.

The hardest bulls to ride are rock hard, big, super athletic and smart. They have the ability to buck you off in either direction, and have a lot of jump and kick. I put bulls like Burns Rodeo's Mr. T, the 1986 PRCA Bucking Bull of the Year, in this category. If he felt you an inch to the inside, he might keep moving to the outside to get you dropped off in the well, or he might change directions on you. If he felt you an inch to the outside, he might tighten up his turnback, speed it up or move around there a little harder. The great bulls are smart. They know where you are at all times, and do whatever it takes to try to get you on the ground. Other bulls are dumb. They'll have a guy bucked off and jump right back underneath him. It makes you wonder what they're thinking.

Horses are a little different than bulls. They don't try to throw you off the same way as a bull. A great bronc, like Calgary Stampede's Lonesome Me (Skoal), is big, strong, smart and athletic, and also has the ability to jump high into the air, kick and drop. He'll leap three feet in the air and take you with him, then he'll throw his head back and make you feel like you're riding with no hands because you're suddenly riding with a loose rein.

The great bareback horses, like (Powder River Rodeo's) Khadafy Skoal, and (Franklin Rodeo's) Skoal's Airwolf, have a lot of the same traits as the rank saddle broncs. They're big, strong and athletic, and they jump, kick and drop really hard. They also change leads every jump, which jerks you back and forth, and makes it hard to stay square.

But the buckers come in all shapes and sizes. Show me the 10 best horses and bulls of all time, and I'll show you 10 totally different animals. They'll be different sizes, shapes, colors and personalities. Bulls like (Beutler and Son's) Cowtown and (Dan Russell's) Skoal's Pacific Bell wanted to kill somebody. (Donnie Kish and John Growney's) Red Rock was so gentle that you could go in the pen and take a nap on him. Two of the horses I retired on my ranch, (Dell Hall, then Harry Vold's) Alibi and (Harry Vold's) Rusty were both great broncs, but had opposite appearances. Alibi was huge and strong; Rusty looked like a little canner. They're proof that looks mean nothing.

93

THE MENTAL GAME

I either win something or learn something every time I ride. There's a lesson in every victory and every defeat.

One of the most important skills you can learn in rodeo is the ability to go back, think through each ride, and recognize what went right or wrong and why. When you've never ridden before it's common to totally black out when the gate opens. Fear and adrenaline have that effect on people. But after awhile, when each part of the ride starts to feel more familiar, you progress to where each ride becomes more of a blur. In time, you learn to relive a ride clearly; to focus and analyze every move. At this point in my career, after thousands of rides in all three roughstock events, everything happens for me in slow motion. I can even anticipate some things, like what a horse or bull's next move will be, before they happen, because I've been in just about every situation imaginable.

If I get thrown off these days, I know exactly why. There isn't a time, now, when a bull just bucks too hard. That's never a good enough explanation for why I got bucked off. If I'm doing my part just right, they can't buck me off. But there are times when a bull might make a move that causes me to make a mistake.

To become mentally strong, I've had to learn to take those mistakes and figure out what I could have done differently to counteract each move. I think about how I'll react differently, when the same situation presents itself again, and put a different reaction into my subconscious for next time. Then I clean the slate and go on, so that I can ride with a clear head. I think about those things after they happen, and before I ride again, because there's no time to think during a ride; only time to react. That's why I don't use visualization techniques or mental imaging before each ride — how

<(Tim Mantoani photo)

can you visualize what hasn't happened yet? It doesn't work for me. I have to deal with each situation as it arises. I don't know what a bronc or bull's going to do before he does it.

It's important in every event to try as hard the last few seconds of a ride as the first. If things are going great when I'm six seconds into a ride, I don't quit hustling and just hang on for the whistle. I won't be as many points that way, and it's a good way to get bucked off and hurt. Even after the whistle blows, I keep riding until I have a chance to make my exit and get away on my feet.

I'm not into all the mental games so many people play with themselves in rodeo and other professional sports. I don't believe you should have to talk yourself into getting excited about something you truly love, so I don't want to spend all my time thinking about what I ought to be thinking about.

I'm not a big goal-setter, either. I never start a year saying, "This year I want to win $250,000 and qualify for the Finals in three events." And I laugh when I hear the advice, "Set attainable goals." What does that mean? I don't get it. I try to do my very best — and pull out all the stops — every day, every rodeo, every ride. I try to win first every time the gate opens, and ride better every time I get on. What else is there to say? What more can you do? If I can do that, I never get sidetracked or lose sight of anything. It gives me a simple, day-to-day, ride-to-ride task — to try to win every single time. I give it everything I have today — every day. I never settle for less than all I've got. Period.

Another piece of advice I've never understood is that you should always write your goals down. That makes me laugh. What a joke. You're in trouble if you can't remember your lifelong dream. If that's the case, maybe you need to re-evaluate the situation. Are you riding because that's all you care about in the world, or are you riding to impress your girlfriend? Are you riding because you want to be the very best you can be at any cost, or because your dad wishes he'd done it? Follow *your* dreams, whatever they are.

When it comes to the psychological side of rodeo, I'm in favor of whatever works. I know the mental end of this game can make me or break me, but believe in a simple, common-sense approach. Some people study and analyze it, but that's just not my way. My mom got me one of those positive-thinking books when I was a kid, and I knew then that it wasn't for me. But I had already had so much experience behind me that confidence wasn't a problem. If *Psycho-Cybernetics* gives you what *you* need, great. In my case, a book like that would probably do me the most good if I taped it to my face and used it as a shield between me and the bull. I don't go for that stuff, but that doesn't make it wrong. If it works for you, go for it.

I don't sweat the small stuff, and I don't lie to myself. When I have the flu, I don't try to tell myself that I feel great. I wouldn't believe it, and that would be lying. But sick or not, I'm still going to try my heart out when that gate opens — a fever or headache damn sure isn't enough to get in the way of that. The main thing is to learn what mental state you perform best in. Then you have to learn how to get there every day, regardless of whether you draw the easiest or rankest bull, whether it's pouring rain or 110 degrees outside, or whether you're riding for $500 or $50,000.

After finding that mental state and figuring out how to get there automatically every time, the key is maintaining it. The guys who can do that are the guys who can shoot the three-point game-winning shot at the buzzer, or ride the bull of the year in the 10th round of the National Finals Rodeo for the world championship. It took me a long time to get there, and not trying too hard or trying the wrong way are still things I work on.

In every event, it's important to remember that everybody started riding sometime. None of us were born knowing how to ride or were handed anything. I can guarantee you that I've hit the ground more than you have, because I've hit the ground more than anyone. How many times you've plowed the arena with your nose isn't the question. What matters is how bad you want it. If you're just learning how to ride and tend to eat a lot of dirt, don't be embarrassed. We've all been there, and that's how we learn.

No one just lucks out and finds themselves at the National Finals one day because they've been dreaming about it. Everybody wants the magic trick; the secret to success. But there isn't one. The guy who tries the hardest and listens the hardest has the edge. All kinds of body types and styles have worked over the years, but trying hard no matter what the circumstances is the one thing all champions have in common.

"Try" is the single most important factor in this game. A lot of guys can ride, and everybody rides a little differently. So the guys who work the hardest, push themselves hardest and want it the most win. That's why trying is everything. Tuff Hedeman, Lane Frost, Cody Lambert, Jim Sharp and Clint Branger dominated for so long because of their try. I try hard like that, too, because it works.

Try is something I've had since I was 2 years old. I'm sure some of it was natural. Both my parents try hard at everything they do. They also raised me to believe that if I tried hard enough I could do anything. So I learned to have high expectations of myself early on in life. The most important things I learned from my dad were not the mechanics of riding, but his attitude. He didn't teach it to me; I learned it just by spending time with him.

What took me a long time to figure out was learning how to try the right way — to stay fluid, relaxed and focused while trying as hard as I can. Before I figured that out, I was stiff, my mind wasn't clear and I was forcing things. It's the difference between trying to hit a baseball over the fence and just swinging through it. You'll hit more balls out of the park by staying relaxed, focused and fluid, and just swinging through. If you don't believe me, ask Mark McGwire. He didn't set the Major League home run record in 1999 by aiming for the upper decks.

When I was a kid, bull riding was the event I wanted to win the most. I thought I should've won big in it at the 5-year-old level, but I didn't win a national championship in bull riding until I was in college. That's when I finally realized how to direct all my energy, and how much a clear mind helps when it comes to going the distance.

"Trying right" is something everyone needs to learn for himself; in his own way. Bucking off a bull in the short round at the National High School Finals Rodeo in 1986 and '87, when I was in a position to win a national title, were two of the worst moments of my life at the time. But now, when I look back on those times, I realize they made some of my greatest moments possible. They taught me things that helped me win world titles at the professional level. That's when I learned the difference between trying hard and forcing things, and trying hard and letting myself ride the way I know I can.

I can't see one aspect of getting nervous that's helpful. If I'm nervous, I'm tense. And when I'm tense, I don't ride my best. There's a big difference between being nervous and using the butterflies that come with that adrenaline pump to my advantage. When I'm relaxed I let it hang out more, and stretch my talents to the edge.

I've had two shots at the Calgary Stampede's $50,000 showdown-round bonus in the bull riding that are perfect examples. One year earlier in my career I had a good chance, and I tensed up and choked. In 1998, with the advantage of that experience behind me, I was relaxed, calm and confident, and got the job done. I learned from a defeat, turned things around and got a victory out of it. My mental frame of mind made the difference between total frustration and stepping up on stage in front of 30,000 fans, fireworks flying, to the tune of Tina Turner's "Simply the Best" blaring across the sound system, to pick up a gigantic cardboard check worth $50,000.

97

I'm three times as busy behind the chutes as most guys who only work one event. But I ride better when I stay loose and relaxed. The trick for me is to get through all the stress of getting ready for the next event in a calm, orderly manner, and having my equipment organized. I don't ever want to make things more hectic for myself than they already are.

Visiting with my friends keeps me relaxed between events. This is my job, but I don't want it to feel that way. I ride better when I'm in a fun mood. When it comes time to get down into that chute I'm all business. But there's a big difference between tight and focused, and it's the difference between winning and losing.

At a rodeo that's well-run, I move along from one event to the next with no spare time, which suits me fine. I get in a groove, and roll with it. I even like rerides sometimes because it gives me that extra obstacle to overcome. I wouldn't want to take a bareback riding reride during the saddle bronc riding and then jump right on a bronc every day, but I don't mind doing it sometimes because it's a challenge. I'd been saying "Just do it" long before Nike made a slogan out of it. That's how I've always looked at life — excuses don't cut it. The name of this game is to ride every horse or bull you draw the best you possibly can. If you do that on a consistent basis, there's no stopping you.

Rodeo's just like most things in life — it isn't "fair." A fair has a Ferris wheel, and happens in the spring. So many things happen to every cowboy who rodeos that are "unfair" and beyond anyone's control. Your car can break down and leave you stranded in the desert in the middle of the night on the way to the rodeo. A bull can run you down the gate or fall on top of you. Being a cowboy means gritting your teeth, stepping up and doing whatever it takes to overcome whatever gets in your way. When I get thrown off, it's my fault. Period. Because it doesn't matter what a horse or bull does. If I execute all my basic steps perfectly, I can ride Godzilla.

What separates the good cowboys from the greats in my mind is that the greats ante up all their chips every time; not just when it's easy to do it. They love to ride, and it shows. That's something the cowboy greats have in common with the best horses and bulls, which are the kind I love to draw. Getting on them is why I'm in this sport. I've learned how to make butterflies work for me, because that almost scared feeling is what makes it possible for me to ride the High Chaparrals (owned by Mike Cervi) and Gunslingers (David Bailey). Because I know that if I give it all I've got, I can ride them. I don't turn on the adrenaline until I scoot up to nod. Then it hits me like goose bumps.

I rise to the occasion when I draw the best horse or bull in the herd. I don't get any more scared or nervous when I draw a Red Wolf (Herrington Cattle Company), Mister T (Hal Burns) or Pacific Bell (Dan Russell) than when I just have a nice one, because if I execute it perfectly, my style will work on any bull or horse in the world. Legends are made when the best guys draw the best bulls; when you ride the unrideable. I can't even begin to explain what it felt like to be 90 points on Gunslinger in Nashville, at the 1994 Professional Bull Riders Bullnanza event, or 93.5 on Red Wolf at the 1998 Jerome Davis Challenge in Charlotte, N.C., and have thousands of people give me a standing ovation. There's no other feeling on earth like that; when on that given day you might have been the only guy in the world who could ride that bull.

When the best horse or bull in the herd shows up next to their name, the champions start licking their chops. They're the guys who turn up the adrenaline and the intensity when they draw the best one. The feeling they get when they ride a bucker is the whole reason they rodeo. It might sound a little cruel to say that I think a big reason a lot of guys don't win when they draw the best bulls and horses is because they're scared. But it's true. They'll usually have several excuses for why it didn't work, but a lot of times their fear gets them down.

Relaxing and focusing behind the chutes before a bull ride in Tucson, Arizona. (Cowpix photo)

Cuttin' up with my friends, like Ted Nuce (left) and Joe Baumgartner (right) at the San Jose Firefighters Rodeo, keeps tension from building. If you're nervous, you won't ride your best. (Cowpix Photo)

Those same guys complain all the time because they say they never draw good. That makes me sick. There will be times in every cowboy's career when he draws all good, or all bad, for a month. It's happened to all of us. But when you rodeo hard for a full year, you put your name in the hat the same as everyone else and it all weighs out. Bitching about things you can't control doesn't change them — not the draw, not the judges, not PROCOM (the PRCA's central entry system, which randomly draws stock and positions — when you're up at each rodeo — on a computer system). If the judges say you missed a horse out and you didn't, they aren't going to change it in their books if you gripe.

Even when I draw a dink, I always try to make the very best ride I can on every animal. I ride every horse or bull like he's the best one I ever got on, and it's really important

to do that. It keeps me sharp and keeps me trying. And that way, I'm ready when I do get a good one. I get really mad at myself when I catch myself riding ho-hum on a dink. That makes me feel like a dink. Because if I'm not aggressive and doing things 100 percent right, I might not be ready when I draw that great one.

The good ones don't come along every day, and you don't get "overs" when you mess one up. It's hard to maintain that kind of intensity every day, but you have to. You can pick up a lot of third- and fourth-place checks along the way if you ride the mediocre animals great. That's just part of consistent riding.

I have a lot of respect for a lot of guys in rodeo. One of them is 1992, '96, '99 and 2000 World Champion Saddle Bronc Rider Billy Etbauer, because he only goes down one

*Putting a new pad on my bull rope. I always use the best equipment, and
I never use my equipment as an excuse. (David Jennings photo)*

Staying loose behind the chutes with Mark Cain. (Cowpix photo)

way, and that's with both barrels blazing. He goes for first at any cost, every time. He tries so hard to be great, and he never plays it safe and just hangs on. I admire that trait so much and try to live by it myself. Even though he's one of the great bronc riders, I've seen Billy hit the ground as much as anyone. But I've never, ever seen him safety up. I've seen him be two feet out of the saddle and headed for the ground, and the last thing he does is reach up there with his feet to take a pass at one more spur stroke. He's not afraid to hit the ground; to open up and try to be 90 points or mud. I love that about him.

Intimidation is an obstacle for most people, especially when they crack out at the professional level. When I first came around in the PRCA I wasn't intimidated, but that was because I was wanting to show the big boys that I could ride, too. I had respect for guys like Lane, Tuff, Jim, Cody and Clint, but wasn't intimidated by them when I was 17 because I'd already been through so much by then. I'd been on as many bulls and horses as a lot of 30-year-old veterans by then.

Jealousy is an emotion I don't understand in any form, but most people, including me, have to deal with it one way or another. Some of the people who aren't willing to pay the price and want success handed to them are jealous of people who have made it. Once you've made it there are times people don't treat you well because they're jealous or resentful of what you've accomplished. That's just human nature, I guess. I don't feel jealous of anyone, because I know I'm giving it everything I have. I'm satisfied with doing *my* very best because that's as good as it gets for anyone. People who are jealous need to get their own ball rolling. If they worked hard enough to feel good about themselves they wouldn't dislike other people for doing it.

I'd always like to say, "Don't ever quit." But that'd be bad advice if it wasn't mixed with common sense. I don't want a kid who looks up to me to hang on when he's

under a bull's belly and get hurt. Giving it all you've got is one thing. But when the game's over, make a safe exit — even if it is before the whistle. Weathering a life-threatening storm isn't going to win you anything and it can get you killed.

When I ante up and hang in there when things are looking bad is when I feel that with a great last-ditch effort and some never-say-die moves, there's a chance. I don't do it if I feel like I'm really just setting myself up to get hurt.

I believe in the Code of the West. What goes around comes around. Western justice. Nobody gets special treatment, and you get what you earn. That's how I live my life and that's how I go about my rodeo business. It doesn't pay to cheat or whine. It does pay to work hard and try your heart out.

I like to get to a rodeo two hours before it starts so I have time to get in a relaxed mood after the rat race that goes along with all the traveling we do. After being wound up from the plane ride or wild drive in the rental car, I let all the pressure out by visiting, laughing and joking around with my friends.

Then I get myself in a little different frame of mind for each event. In my mind, the guy with the most try, who'll give it all he's got at any cost, wins in the bareback riding. When things get wild, he's the guy who'll rise up and get a little wilder. So I like to get my motor running in the bareback riding. I get fired up, because the most aggressive guy wins. I think an aggressive attitude is 80 percent of bareback riding.

I like to stay more relaxed in the saddle bronc and bull riding, because I think control and learning how to try the right way, as I mentioned earlier, is a lot more important in them. In the saddle bronc riding, it's important to be relaxed because you're matching moves with the horse and always striving for perfect form.

103

While it's usually a question of how well you can ride a horse, the trick to riding bulls is staying on. Being relaxed in the bull riding helps because you need to keep a clear head in order to react to what a bull does; to handle all the unpredictable variables that make it so hard to ride a bull for eight seconds. Bull riding is full of hills, when you don't think there's a bull in the world that can throw you off, and valleys, when you don't think there's a bull you can ride. But because it's so hard just to make the whistle in the bull riding, a game plan won't do you much good. And because the degree of difficulty is so high, thinking of bull riding in basic terms is the best frame of mind.

Slumps and rolls (hot streaks) are a never-ending battle in rodeo, and I deal with them just like everyone else. This isn't a sport where once you're on top you stay there. To stay at the top of my game I have to work at it every day. Without that kind of consistent dedication you can't make it in rodeo, or anything else for that matter, for any length of time.

Cody and I were at a rodeo one time and I was helping him get on his bull. I was pulling his rope and he was taking his wrap. I told him, "Do whatever it takes to stay on." About 20 people started cracking up laughing. But that's the way we look at it. Where other people would have been saying, "Reach" or "Keep your chin down," I said, "Do whatever it takes to stay on." Everybody thought I was trying to be funny, but that's the kind of attitude that Cody and I went at it with. When we traveled together, from my rookie year in 1988 until Cody retired

Waiting. (Cowpix Photo)

at the end of 1996, we'd always say something to loosen each other up when times were getting tense. That's why together we were stronger.

I will never give up on trying to improve as long as I continue to ride. For one, you can always be better than you are — I don't care who you are. And for two, you have to try to get better just to stay as good as you are in this game. It's a constant battle in rodeo. One day you can be 92 points; the next day you can fall off of one you could have ridden when you were 12.

You can't fake love. And you can't be great at anything without loving it. Michael Jordan loves to play basketball and it shows. Troy Aikman loves to play football and it shows. Rodeo greats are no different. Jim Shoulders, Larry Mahan and Roy Cooper are legends in this sport because they love the game. To be great you have to be willing to do whatever it takes to win; to crave the challenge of an unrideable bull or an unbeatable time.

When I was a kid, I roped calves and team roped. I liked those events, and it showed. I loved the riding events, and that showed. I won a little in the timed events and I won a lot in the riding events. I slept, ate and drank riding bulls and bucking horses.

I don't think in any sport or anything else in life you're going to find a champion that doesn't absolutely love what he's doing. You can tell. It's too hard. There's too much that goes into being a champion not to love it.

104

I probably have been blessed with some ability, but there's a lot more to making it than riding well. There's the mental strain, the physical strain, the ups, the downs, the getting beat and losing. But there's nothing worthwhile in life that isn't hard to get. When things are easy, they're not as gratifying. That's how everything in the world is. That's why diamonds are worth what they're worth — they're hard to come by. If they were laying all over the ground like rocks they wouldn't be worth anything.

I love to draw an animal people think can't be ridden. It's not much different from bringing the field-goal kicker in with one second left in the Super Bowl. If he makes it, his team wins. If he doesn't, the whole season's out the window. Having the control and strength to come through in the clutch is the difference between great and good; man and boy; champion and chump.

The great cowboys are the ones with the biggest hearts. They're the guys who try the hardest and ante up all their chips every time; not just when it's easy or popular to do it. They don't care how pretty they look. They try their guts out and do whatever it takes to win. That might include gritting it out when they're so sore they can hardly walk or hanging on the side of a bull the last two seconds and giving it a last-ditch effort because they're so determined to win at any cost.

Even when we lose, we all need to try to remember to be grateful for everything we have. I'm especially reminded of that when I meet kids with brain tumors or birth defects. Kids like that break my heart, and amaze me. They smile and are happy anyway. They don't complain or ask why. They just live each day and have fun.

There are times in July when every cowboy gets tired — when we miss home, our families, our own beds, our dogs and home-cooked meals. That's when we need to stop and count our blessings. That's when I remember that I'm not punching a clock at some boring job I hate, or worse. Guys like Lane Frost, Brent Thurman and Glen Keeley are gone forever. What would they give to have our problems?

CHEATING DEATH

Danger is a big part of this game, and there are two ways of looking at it. On one hand, rodeo wouldn't be what it is without it. If there was no danger factor involved, a lot of cowboys and fans wouldn't love it like they do because it wouldn't be the sport it is. Sponsors are attracted to dangerous sports for the same reason. You don't see many major corporations chasing chess players. It all goes back to the days of gladiators and knights in shining armor. People are drawn to danger. They're intrigued by it.

The fact is, rodeo isn't checkers. When cowboys climb down on a bull or bronc at the NFR, they get the same kind of adrenaline pump speed skiers get when their skis are pointed straight down a mountain at 120 miles per hour at the Olympics; the same charge race-car drivers get when they're doing 220 miles an hour at the Indy 500.

On the other hand, cowboys realize that every time they put their hand in the riggin' or bull rope, or every time they crawl into the saddle their lives are on the line. It doesn't matter how good they ride or how long they've been riding, no one is immune to rodeo's danger factor. There are too many uncontrollable variables involved, and there's no way to predict or change what a 2,000-pound bull might decide to do on any given day.

Most people don't realize just how strong bulls are. I've seen them jump six-foot fences. I saw a bull jump the fence at the coliseum in Phoenix one year, and he got up on the concourse full of scattering people. I saw that happen in El Paso, too. What a wreck. I've seen a bull throw a 200-pound clown barrel, with a 200-pound clown in it, over a six-foot fence with his head — just with his neck strength. Sometimes when they're loading bulls on the trucks you'll see a bull stick his head up

< Bull riding ain't all sunglasses and swimming pools. (Louise Serpa Photo)

Lane Frost with Red Rock and one of his owners, John Growney. (Sue Rosoff Photo)

under the bull in front of him, that weighs a ton, and lift him up. Harry Vold's famous one-horned fighting bull, Crooked Nose, once stuck his horn into a big round bale of hay that weighed about 1,200 pounds, and lifted it up with that horn. A 150-pound man is like an ant to a bull, and bulls are mean by nature.

Brent Thurman was a great friend of mine. Brent died right after the NFR in 1994, from injuries he suffered when his 10th-round bull stepped on his head. There's no sicker feeling in the world than seeing something like that happen to one of your friends right in front of your eyes.

I met Brent in 1988 in Dayton, Ohio, at the first PRCA rodeo I ever went to. He was one of the funniest guys I've ever been around. He always kept the mood light behind the chutes. When I'd get bucked off and mad, Brent could always make me laugh with the funny stuff he said. He helped me remember that it isn't the end of the world to buck off a bull.

I was sitting on a pickup horse in the arena when Lane Frost died at the 1989 Cheyenne Frontier Days Rodeo. After a winning ride, his bull hit him in the back with a horn. I've always gotten on a horse and helped with things, like running horses and bulls out of the arena, after I ride at Cheyenne. When Lane got hit I turned to ride off and clear the arena because it didn't look like any big deal. I thought he'd get up and walk away from it. But he didn't. They tried to revive him, but Lane died right there in the arena of internal injuries.

Lane had the same kind of effect on me as Brent as far as making me laugh. There were times I got drilled, and while I was staggering to get to my feet I'd look up and see Lane — in the arena, laughing, pointing at me and slapping his leg. Lane also taught me a lot about riding bulls. We talked about it all the time, and I watched him ride every chance I got. To this day I watch the videotape he made, "Bull Talk," because I think he had a lot of good ideas about riding and I like to remind myself of them.

Glen Keeley died March 24, 2000 at my PBR Bud Light Cup event, the Ty Murray Invitational, in Albuquerque, New Mexico. Glen, who was the 1989 Canadian champion bull rider, started a great ride on Terry Williams' 1999 PBR Bucking Bull of the Year, Promise Land. But a little over halfway into the ride, Promise Land jerked him down. His hand hung an extra split-second in his rope, which jerked him down underneath Promise Land, who weighs about 2,000 pounds. Promise Land stepped right in the middle of Glen's chest, which severed his liver. Glen died that night of massive internal injuries.

Glen's family, including five brothers who've all ridden bulls, took a lot of comfort from the fact that Glen died riding bulls and not in a car accident or some other meaningless way. Like one brother, Jayson, who was in a coma with severe head injuries for a couple weeks back in 1994 after a wreck at the PRCA rodeo in Caldwell, Idaho, said, "By God, he went out doing what he loved and he was on top of the world. Glen went out in a blaze of glory. What else can you ask for in this world than to die doing what you love?"

I've known this sport was dangerous since I was 2 years old. So losing Brent, Lane and Glen were painful reminders of what I already knew — that it can happen to any of us at any time. It can happen to great cowboys and great people. Brent, Lane and Glen were heroes to a lot of little kids. They were and still are inspirations to a lot of people, including me.

Lane and Brent were only 25 when they died. Glen had just turned 30. They had short lives, but great ones. A cowboy would rather live 25 years doing what he loves and being his own boss than 100 years at some miserable job he can't stand. I know those guys felt that way.

So did Jerome Davis, who was the 1995 PRCA world champion bull rider. Like Lane, Brent and Glen, Jerome rode as well as anybody. He's a great guy, too. But bulls aren't picky. They don't discriminate when choosing a victim. In

109

In a jam at the NFR. (PRCA Photo by Dan Hubbell)

March 1998, at Tuff Hedeman's Championship Challenge in Fort Worth (a PBR Bud Light Cup event), Jerome hit heads with Jerry Nelson's Knock 'em Out John. Jerome was unconscious when he hit the ground, so he had no chance to break his fall. Jerome's now paralyzed from the chest down.

It's easy to see why bull riding has for years been voted the world's most dangerous sport by sports writers. The stakes are high in this game. There's no higher price to pay than your life or your ability to walk. But it's what we love. And the fact is, driving and flying to all the rodeos is just as dangerous as what we do once we get there. But that's part of the game, too.

Just ask World Champion Bareback Riders (and brothers) Marvin and Mark Garrett, bronc rider Scott Johnston, and bull rider Thad Bothwell. They wrecked (five-time World Champion Saddle Bronc Rider and 1997

World Champion All-Around Cowboy) Dan Mortensen's plane on the way to the Cow Palace, which is the last regular-season rodeo of the year, in November 1998. They were headed to San Francisco to try to gather up a few last-minute points before the NFR, and they crashed and burned. Marvin, Thad and Scott broke their backs, among other serious injuries, and their pilot, Johnny Morris, died. If Mark hadn't been able to drag them all out of there, they would have gone up in flames with the plane. There was nothing left when the smoke cleared. But what's probably most amazing about the way we travel is that it doesn't happen more often. We're always trying to get places faster than is safe. Speed limits don't apply to cowboys.

The danger's there in every event, though the life-threatening injuries usually come up at the roughstock end of the arena. Duane Daines, the great Canadian saddle bronc riding and all-around champion who rode at the NFR nine times, was paralyzed in September 1995, when a bronc flipped on him in the chute. Like I said before, danger doesn't dodge great cowboys. It's part of their lives, too; something everyone in rodeo has to deal with sooner or later to some degree.

And contrary to what I believed when I was 18 — that injuries were for other guys — it's a fact of life that applies to me, too. My mom always taught me not to take anything for granted, including my health, and I've learned to appreciate what good advice that is. I've actually been pretty lucky not to have more serious injuries in my career, considering how many bucking horses and bulls I've been on since I was 2.

I think being alert and keeping your head will get you through a lot of binds in rodeo. There are times when the outcome is beyond your control — when things go bad so fast there's nothing you can do — but the ability to think instead of panic will save you in a lot of those situations.

Lewis Field, who won three world all-around championships from 1985-87 and the 1985 and '86 world bareback riding titles, had his hand bound in his riggin' once and some idiot rolled his horse ahead. Most guys would have panicked right before they got clotheslined and knocked out by the bar those gates slide on. Not Lewis. In that split second he laid flat back, rode that horse into the next chute, sat back up and nodded for him. A guy can go a long way if that little stuff doesn't get in his way and slow him down.

I was 9 the first time I got hurt. It was at a junior rodeo in Globe, Arizona, and it was the second bull I'd ever been on. I was entered in the boys steer riding, but the stock contractor had brought bulls for us to ride. It was the first time that had happened, so I had to do some tall talking to get my dad to let me get on my first bull, an 1,800-pound brindle with big horns. He wasn't exactly what my dad had in mind for his 9-year-old kid who was small for his age.

I was extra excited when I won the "steer" riding that day. But I didn't get so lucky in the second round. I got bucked off six or seven seconds into the ride, then I got stepped on. I didn't cry or get knocked out. But I remember my dad running out there to me with tears streaming down his cheeks because he could see that my bottom teeth — my brand new permanent teeth — were laid back flat in my mouth. I was more worried about reassuring him that I was OK and that it really didn't hurt that bad than I was about myself.

When X-rays showed that my jaw was broken, they wired my mouth shut. I lived on milkshakes and blended foods — my mom ran dinner through the Osterizer every night — until I came back two months later at the state finals. I was in a position to win the whole deal, but was scared after that last go-round. Ironically, that's when it clicked for me to start using my feet to ride. My dad had been trying to tell me how much easier it would be to ride with my feet *and* arms, but I was resisting the feet part. That day at the state finals, with my mouth still wired shut, was the first time I really turned my toes out and got ahold of a steer with my feet.

I drew a big white-and-yellow paint steer that really bucked. He was getting so high in the air that he cleared the clown barrel. After the whistle, I ran back across that arena so excited, yelling, "Dad, I kept my feet in him! I kept my feet in him!" I'm sure I was hard to understand with my mouth wired shut, but my dad knew exactly what I was saying. I didn't care about winning that rodeo — what my dad had been trying to pound into my head about my feet had finally clicked. After that day we never talked about my feet again.

When I was 16, I broke my collarbone when one of Walt Alsbaugh's new practice horses tried to jump out of the arena with me. It was at a little practice arena about a mile and a half down the road from our house in Deer Valley, Arizona. He got hung up on the fence and flipped

111

over backwards on me. But I was young and tough. A few weeks later, I was back in business.

I had my share of bumps, bruises and sore muscles along the way like everyone else, but I didn't break another bone until I was a couple years into my professional career. I broke a bone in my elbow at the 1990 Redding (California)

I've had my share of close calls, where I walked away from ugly looking wrecks that could just as easily have ended my career. There was the time at the 1990 NFR when one of Donnie Gay's horses, Bo, flipped over backwards, right on top of me, coming out of the chute in the ninth round. The swell of my saddle smashed down

Dan Russell's White Lightning threw me off right at the whistle (NFR '92), and my hand hung up a jump. He was trying so hard to hook me before his feet even hit the ground that he landed flat on his side. (Dan Hubbell photo courtesy of Buckers, Inc.)

Rodeo when my foot hung in the stirrup an extra split-second when I was getting bucked off my bronc. It was just long enough to whip me down underneath him, and his hoof grazed and cut my head. Besides breaking a little bone in my elbow, I tore some muscles in my riding arm. I took two months off and came back at Reno that June, where I won the bronc riding.

Wrecks and injuries happen so fast in rodeo. You get about as much warning as when you're driving down the road and there's that split second when you think somebody's about to hit you. You don't have time to react or do anything more than think to yourself, "Oh God, here it comes."

on my right knee, with all that horse's weight behind it. I was lucky to get out of there with nothing more than a severely bruised and swollen knee. I had to sit out the rest of that round and the 10th round, but it obviously could have been much worse. A lot of people expected me to be mad about that, because I was sitting good in the averages when it happened and I could have won quite a bit more if I could have finished out the last two rounds. But a fall like that can kill you, and I knew it. I was satisfied with the rodeo I had at the Finals that year, because I tried my hardest and did the best I could with what I was dealt. I knew that wasn't the last rodeo they were ever going to have.

After that two-month timeout at the end of 1990 and first of 1991, I rolled along injury-free for a while. But like they always say in rodeo, it isn't *if* you'll get hurt, but *when* and how bad.

The first time I hurt my left knee was at a 1991 bull riding event in Odessa, Texas. There was an arena outside a little bar there called Dos Amigos. I was riding in a benefit bull riding for a guy who'd gotten hurt. I rode my bull, pulled my wrap and stepped off perfectly, on both feet. My left knee popped when I hit the ground, but I figured I'd just sprained it. No such luck. I'd torn the anterior cruciate ligament in half. The doctors told me I had two choices: get it fixed then or rehabilitate it and try to get by as long as possible. I picked door number two, so I took two months off and rehabilitated it. It was sore when I rode, but I kept going.

In 1994, at the Southwestern Exposition and Livestock Show and Rodeo in Fort Worth, a bull ran me down the gate and twisted the heck out of my right leg. I thought he tore it off. I didn't realize until June 1995 how bad that injury really was. The doctors thought then that the medial collateral ligament was all that had been torn. But we later learned that the posterior cruciate ligament was almost torn in half, too. I finished it off at the Professional Bull Riders Bud Light Cup event in Rancho Murieta, California.

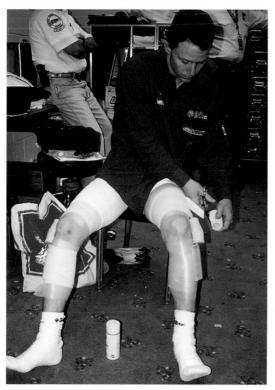

Prepping my knees for the braces before a ride. (Kendra Santos Photo)

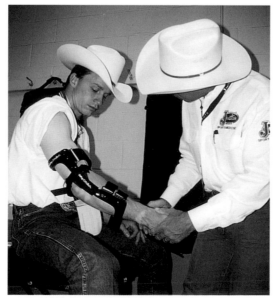

Dr. Tandy Freeman fits a brace on me after I hyper-extended my riding arm elbow in July '99. The injury kept me out two months. (Kendra Santos Photo)

June 17, 1995 was one of the most miserable days of my life. I felt my knee pop during my short-round ride but, since it's impossible to shut adrenaline off like the faucet in the kitchen sink, I kept riding 'til I heard the whistle. It's just not natural to jump off before the whistle. I was 86 points on my bull and placed in the round. But when I hit the ground and tried to get up I knew I was in trouble. I couldn't do it. My right knee felt like it had come out of joint.

I'll never forget laying there in that hot little mosquito tent — a makeshift locker room — behind the chutes. My leg was throbbing so bad I wished it would fall off. The Justin SportsMedicine guys got ice on it immediately, and put me on a muscle stimulator machine to get the circulation going in it in an attempt to keep the swelling down.

Dr. Tandy Freeman, my great friend and the best orthopedic surgeon in the world, was there to confirm my worst suspicions: reconstructive knee surgery was no longer optional. It hurt so bad, but I think I dreaded the phone call to my parents even more. I knew they'd be sad, and I hated to hurt them.

I guess word got around there pretty fast that it didn't look too good, because all the cowboys and staff people kept walking up with funny looks on their faces as if to

113

say they were sorry and really didn't know what to say. Maybe they knew there was nothing they could say that was going to make me feel a whole lot better.

Anyone who imagines life behind the chutes as glamorous should have seen me laying there in my underwear in that dark little tent, with my ice-covered leg stuck in the air. The dirt, manure and sweat made a mud on me. I finally just closed my eyes.

About then I got whacked across the forehead. It was a kid hitting me through a tear in the tent with a poster he wanted me to sign. At times like that, when a guy wants to be alone and anonymous, it's hard to be gracious. Two thoughts crossed my mind at the same time. Do I snap and tell this kid to get lost and leave me alone? Probably not a good idea, I figured. Then I'd be as rude as he was. I decided to bite my already fat lip and sign the poster; to be the bigger man, and show

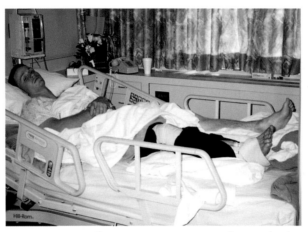

Recuperating from PCL surgery at Baylor Medical Center in 1995. (Butch and Joy Murray Photo)

the obnoxious 9-year-old the definition of poise under pressure. I can only imagine what a professional football or basketball player would have done in that situation, but then again professional athletes in other sports would never be put in that position. They're immediately isolated in a private training room when they get hurt. But rodeo isn't like any other sport. I think it has more trying times to it than the others. But I think they're worth it.

Tandy, who's the director of medical services for the Justin SportsMedicine Team, spent the afternoon with me, and by that night I knew, based on his evaluation of the situation, that I needed major surgery.

Tandy reconstructed the posterior cruciate ligament in my right knee in Dallas on June 30, 1995. It took four hours and was pretty major surgery, but I walked out of

there on crutches two days later. Four days later I threw the crutches away.

I knew I had some time off and a serious road of rehab ahead of me, so while I was at it I had the anterior cruciate ligament in my left knee fixed, also in Dallas, on September 5 that same year. The second surgery took two and a half hours, and was a breeze compared to the operation on my right leg. I got up and walked away without crutches the morning after the surgery.

Those surgeries — the first major setbacks of my professional career — taught me how important it is to keep up with therapy and listen to your doctor. You always see guys who try to come back too soon or get out of some of the hard work it takes to come back. But most people aren't smarter than their doctors. They know what's best for you, so I listened to mine.

The time off after the knee surgeries was actually good for me. I would never choose to be hurt, and wish it had never happened, but if it had to happen it came at a good point in my career. I'd been rodeoing hard my whole life; almost ridiculously hard the seven and a half years before the surgeries. I think I was at a point where a year off did my mind and body some good.

I had a chance to catch up with my life. I was able to spend more time with my family and friends, made a lot of sponsor appearances and caught up on photo shoots for ads. In November 1995, my international fan club — the Ty Murray Fan Club (see tymurray.com) — got kicked off on the side panel of Kellogg's Raisin Bran cereal boxes. Western Pacific Airlines painted a picture of me riding David Bailey's bull Playboy Skoal on the tail of one of their planes.

This very close call was during the seventh performance of the 1992 NFR. I got a horn in the back, but it resulted in just a scrape. Pictures like this make me so glad Cody designed protective vests for cowboys. (PRCA Photo by Mark Reis)

I also got to be the Super Bowl XXX Parade Marshal in Phoenix. Baseball legend Nolan Ryan and I carried the official game ball and coin the last leg of a Pony Express-style delivery to the stadium. The ball and coin started in Holbrook, Arizona, and were handed off to various riders throughout the trek. We took them the last mile, down the streets of downtown Phoenix, horseback at a dead run.

A lot of good things happened to me in the months I was away from rodeo that might not have if I'd been rodeoing. I got to go on an unbelievable pack trip with a bunch of my cowboy friends. We started in Wyoming and rode 23 miles into the Bear Tooth Mountains. We actually camped in Montana. In all those lakes and creeks there were as many trout as we took time to catch.

Everyone expected me to be devastated and heartbroken by the knee injuries. Of course it would have been nice to win the record seventh world all-around championship that year and make it seven in a row, but I didn't have a choice in the matter. The days of trying to "get by" with knees that weren't 100 percent were over. My knees made the decision for me, so I didn't have a tough choice to make. I was needing a break from it all. Part of this lifestyle — mostly all the driving — wears on you after so many years.

Besides, I've always been more concerned with being a good cowboy than specific accomplishments or records. The recovery time after my knee surgeries was the first time in seven years I wasn't sore somewhere. I still craved riding and winning, so I knew I'd do whatever it took to come back when my body was ready. But I was determined to give my knees all the time and therapy they needed to be as good as new before I returned to the arena. And it was great to get away from phones, the noise, the hustle and bustle of the road. I took naps in the grass at my ranch at noon, and sat around campfires with friends. I finally had the time to ride a saddle horse through the country and see fish jumping out of the streams on my ranch with my own eyes.

You can either cry about a year like I had in 1995 or not — I chose not to. I looked at the bright side, and took the time to appreciate all I had to be grateful for. It was also a great lesson in rodeo appreciation. Working hard every day at therapy gave me two hours a day — when my heart and lungs were burning — to ask myself, "How bad do you want it? Is it worth it?" Then I'd grit my teeth and pedal that bike or climb that stair-stepper even faster.

It was a completely foreign feeling when opening day of the 1995 National Finals Rodeo rolled around and I was there to make sponsor appearances and commentate on the ESPN telecast — without my riggin' bag. But I'd prolonged the inevitable as long as possible.

I returned to the arena in the spring of 1996, and it was great to be back. I won about $40,000 at the PBR events the first four weeks I was back, and felt like my old self again. But on April 28, during the short round of PBR's George Paul Memorial Bull Riding in Del Rio, Texas, I tore a ligament in my left (free-arm) shoulder away from the bone. The bull I was riding, Bad Company Rodeo's Bad Moon, was turning back to the right, into my hand, so hard that he tipped me off to the left side. I was using my free arm to get back over in the middle of him. I felt a pain in my shoulder during the ride, but kept riding and ended up winning second. I was sore, but didn't think it was any big deal. The following weekend, I split the win with Jim Sharp at the Jerome Davis Championship Challenge PBR event in Charlotte, North Carolina. The pain kept getting worse with each ride until finally, the weekend after that at the PBR Bud Light Cup event in Birmingham, Alabama, things got really bad. By then, my shoulder felt sore when I was just walking around. When it was up and back, like it has to be to ride a lot of bulls, it felt like somebody was sticking a knife in my shoulder.

Tandy anchored the ligament back to the bone on May 28 in Dallas, and told me to plan on another six months of rehab. I was disappointed, but — just like with my knees

— I knew there was nothing I could do about it. I'm not one to sit around and cry about things I can't fix, because whining doesn't change them. Rodeo taught me to roll with the punches at a young age.

I again worked hard in therapy religiously every day. The sessions included a lot of stretching and some weights. Before long, I could handle chores on the ranch. I could feed the cows and brand the calves, but I still couldn't get my arm back behind my ear and above my shoulder, where I needed it to be when bulls kick and my free arm's way back. All I could do was stay in shape, so when Tandy cleared me I'd be ready to go.

I was more anxious waiting to get to ride again after I hurt my shoulder than I was after I hurt my knees. After the knee surgeries, I was ready for some time off. When it came time to get back to rodeoing I was a little torn, because I'd just bought my ranch and there was so much that needed to be done around there. After the shoulder surgery I got to missing it pretty bad. I was ready to get back to work.

Still, I made the most of the time off. In October, I attended the PBR Finals at the MGM Grand in Las Vegas. I was the MGM's rodeo ambassador at the time. I was also a member of the PBR Board of Directors at that time, so there was a lot of business to take care of there. In November, I spoke to 40,000 kids from all over the country at the National Future Farmers of America Convention, which was held in conjunction with the American Royal Rodeo in Kansas City. It was the third straight year I'd done that, and it was always a fun experience for me.

I commentated on the Wrangler World of Rodeo NFR telecast again in 1996, and also wrote the Ty Murray NFR Report, a daily column that's now annually printed in newspapers and posted on web sites all over the United States. Those were a couple of experiences that helped me appreciate aspects of this sport that I'd never paid any attention to before. But for me, there's no substitute for riding.

After nine months on the injured reserves list, I returned to the arena — again — in January 1997 at the National Western Livestock Show and Rodeo in Denver. My left shoulder felt strong; like nothing had ever happened to it. I got off to a great start at rodeos like Denver, Odessa, Phoenix, San Antonio, El Paso and Fort Worth, where I won the all-around championship. I felt strong in all three events and was having fun. I honestly didn't feel like I'd missed a step in the time I was out. I was excited about riding again. But before the ink dried on all the stories announcing my big comeback, I got kicked in the teeth again.

I dislocated my right (riding-arm) shoulder on February 8 at the PBR Bud Light Cup event in St. Louis. Jerome Robinson's Bar Fly bucked me off, and the damage was done as soon as I hit the ground. I heard it tear when I landed, and jumped up trying to hold my right arm up with my left hand. It was just dangling there all but unattached to my body, and it hurt like hell until Tandy got it back in the socket 40 minutes later. I'd never experienced pain like that before.

Tandy reconstructed my right shoulder March 3 in Dallas, and gave me another six months of intense rehabilitation to look forward to. It was basically a replay of the surgery on my left shoulder, where he had to reattach the ligaments to the bone.

After seven basically injury-free years, it was pretty discouraging to have a third straight season end that way. But I knew pouting wouldn't change anything. When you're hurt you're hurt. You can be mad or sad, or say, "If I was out there, I could do this or that." But none of that matters. My only option was to bear down and work hard to get back to 100 percent. I'd already learned that there are no shortcuts to a full recovery.

By that time, a lot of people were questioning my decision to come back at all. They told me that I had nothing to prove and that maybe God was trying to tell

This was at the 1996 George Paul Memorial PBR Bud Light Cup event in Del Río, Texas. Mack Altizer's Bad Moon was spinning to the right pretty hard, so I was really having to use my free arm to stay in the middle of him. I tore the ligaments in my free arm (left) shoulder on this ride and was out the rest of the year. (David Jennings Photo)

me to hang it up. It probably seemed to them like I'd been around forever, but I was still only 27 years old. And I was still a cowboy. You don't dedicate your life to something then walk away in your prime.

After another seven months of rehab, I started riding again the first week in September at the PBR Bud Light Cup event at the Lazy E Arena in Guthrie, Oklahoma. I felt a little rusty on the first bull I got on, Terry Williams' Gold Dust, and he dusted me. But I got right back in the swing of things after that.

I got on my first bucking horses in November at the rodeo in Kansas City. I drew pretty middle-of-the-road, but didn't feel one bit rusty, which made me feel good. By then, my whole body felt great. But I was a little gun-shy about getting too excited.

I started off the 1998 season fresh and healthy. After all I'd been through, I appreciated my career more than ever. Danger is always part of the deal, and I accept that. That's why I can get paid in a weekend what it takes most people six months to earn sitting at a desk eight hours a day.

In my opinion, the trick is to be honest with yourself and not ride when there's a good chance of permanent damage and you have no chance of winning because you're so sore you can't move. When you're hurt that bad, going on with it isn't the tough thing to do; it's the stupid thing to do.

Cowboys deal with aches, pains, bumps and bruises on a daily basis in rodeo. But by the time you get to the professional level, you should know your body well enough to make the call; to know when you can grit your teeth, tape up, ice down and put the pain aside — and when you can't. You ride through a lot of pain because everything rides on today, and you don't want to sit out because there might not be a tomorrow. But if you quit doing everything that's dangerous, you might as well live in a glass box.

Staying in shape not only helps me ride better, but cuts down on injuries and soreness, too. It also helps me feel better in every way. When I'm physically fit, I feel stronger and faster, and I have more energy for everything I do. I work out because I like to feel good, and because I feel lousy when I'm run-down and tired. When I take good care of myself is when I also have the best possible chance of winning.

I need to take especially good care of myself when I'm riding every day, which sometimes goes on for months. That goes for everything from my fitness level to how my equipment's adjusted. I might have been able to get away with my bareback riggin' not fitting just right when I was in high school, because when you ride once a week you have six days to get over being sore before you have to get on again. But there are times now when I ride in the afternoon, then jump in and out of a small plane and ride again that night. That's why I go out of my way to make sure my body's in the best shape possible, and that my equipment fits just right so it won't hurt me or hinder my performance.

I don't pretend to be an authority on fitness, but I do have a lot of experience with what does and doesn't work for athletes who make a living riding bucking horses and bulls. I've gotten some good advice from doctors, trainers and coaches over the years, and have come up with a training program that works for me. Its foundation is really just a common-sense, healthy lifestyle. I like to stretch and lift weights; Cody does Jane Fonda. Hey, whatever works.

My weight program is a whole-body workout with extra emphasis on the upper body. I don't do as much lifting with my lower body because, while I want my legs to be strong, in shape and flexible, I don't want them to be bulky.

I use light weights and a lot of repetitions in my workouts for the same reason; because I want my body to be supple and lean. Heavier weights and fewer repetitions just add bulk. It takes strength to ride bucking horses

119

Staying in shape not only helps you ride better but can help cut down on injuries, too. (Kendra Santos Photos)

and bulls, but you don't want to be muscle-bound. You may have noticed that most body builders aren't good athletes. That's why.

I've learned over the years that it's important when working out with weights to extend muscles to their full range of motion to keep them flexible, and so they don't contract and get tight. When I do curls, for example, I extend my arms until they're completely straight. That's the position they're in when a bareback horse jumps away from me. I don't care if you weigh 110 pounds and have Arnold Schwarzeneger's arm, there's no way to keep from getting your arm jerked straight when that happens, so I do everything I can think of to prepare my arm for that jerk.

When I'm home, I work out seven days a week. When I do that, I split my muscle groups into two groups and work each group every other day. Building muscle is tearing down old muscle and rebuilding it stronger than it was before. So I rotate days to give my muscles a chance to rebuild themselves between workouts.

I have a weight room at my ranch, and get quite a bit of exercise just working around there. Since I hurt my knees I've also been going to the Nippon Kenpo Dojo (gym) in

Stephenville. Jim Sharp got me into it. Nippon Kenpo is a form of martial arts that gives me an aerobic workout and makes me strong pound-for-pound. It also helps me stay really flexible, which helps me avoid injuries. No weights are involved, and it works on fast-twitch muscle fibers, which gives you explosive strength and quicker reflexes.

When I'm on the road, I find gyms every chance I get. A lot of hotels have gyms in them. But if there's no time or place to lift weights, I make time for some aerobic exercise and stretching, which I can do anywhere, anytime. That's what's so great about Nippon Kenpo. You don't need a special facility or equipment to do it.

There are times when the pace is so hectic that the riding itself and all the stretching I do keep me in shape. It's a matter of doing whatever it takes to stay fit, no matter where I am or what's going on, because I can't do what I do without being in shape.

My gymnastics background has probably helped me as much as the weight lifting over the years. The two things combined have helped me work three events day in and day out, and to avoid torn, sore muscles. I worked out with the gymnastics team all four years in high school.

When I was a junior and senior, I taught the freshmen and sophomores, and practiced three hours a day. The only drawback was that the meets were on the weekends. I tried out every Friday to qualify for that weekend's meet, but only did it as a personal challenge. I wasn't about to miss a rodeo for anything. My mom tried and tried to talk me into competing at a meet, but me and my one-track mind wouldn't hear of it. I regret that now, because I'll never have that chance again. But that was my choice at the time, so I have to live with it.

Gymnastics did a lot for me, even though I didn't compete. It kept me in great shape, and gave me a lot of strength and balance. In my eyes, gymnasts are the greatest athletes in the world pound-for-pound. There's nobody stronger or more flexible, and doing gymnastics makes you catty. It taught me to fly through the air and land on my feet. Doing "Sukaharas" — which are front flips with a half twist and back flip — and front flips with full twists taught me air sense and about controlling my body with my mind.

I liked all the events in gymnastics except the pommel horse. That I didn't like a horse of any kind seems kind of ironic now, but it was the one event that was boring to me. The high bar, parallel bars, rings and floor exercise were all a thrill for me.

As a sport, gymnastics has a lot in common with rodeo, and I'd encourage kids interested in rodeo to try it. Acrobats take easy tricks, like walking the tightrope with a 40-foot pole, and try to make them look hard. Gymnasts take the

Doing Nippon Kenpo to stay in shape between rides in the hotel gym in Reno. (Kendra Santos Photo)

most difficult tricks and try to make them look easy. That's the key to the roughstock events, too.

I played all sports as a kid. I played Pop Warner football and Little League. I wrestled and retired undefeated after three matches. I liked all the sports, and still do. I still enjoy games like tennis and golf, but play them these days for fun and exercise. They aren't my priority. I've never loved any other sport the way I love rodeo.

I get asked a lot, especially by parents, if I think there's an ideal size for roughstock riders. Sure, I think there are optimal body types for rodeo. Personally, I think 5'8" and 160 pounds is a good size for the roughstock events, and I believe it was God-given that I turned out to be this size and not 6'5" and 280 pounds. But I'm not saying you have to be my size. Look at Tuff and Cody (Hedeman is 5'11" and 175 pounds; Lambert is 5'10" and 180 pounds). Whatever size you are, you have to be strong enough to handle your body size; to be strong pound-for-pound like a gymnast. Because nobody's strong enough to outmuscle a bronc or bull. I never tell a kid he's not built right for riding, partly because there's no telling how big he'll be when he grows up, and partly because you can make just about any size work. The only body type that won't work is one that's fat and out of shape.

I always try to eat good, balanced meals when I'm traveling. But the reality is, there are times when I don't have time to eat at all or when I have to grab something

121

when I'm getting gas. In those situations, I have a weakness for Cheez Whiz on Chicken in a Biscuit crackers. But some choices are better than others, even at a gas station, and I try to do my body the favor of going with a relatively healthy choice.

Cafeterias are my favorite restaurants on the road because I can pick out balanced meals and a variety of foods there. I can get something from all the food groups, and get it cooked about any way I like it. My absolute favorite food is Mexican food in New Mexico, but I'm not too picky. I like all kinds of good food.

Water's my main drink. It tastes the best to me, quenches my thirst and makes me feel better than other drinks. It's good for me too, so I drink gallons of it. When I'm rodeoing, there'll be 15 empty water bottles rattling around in my van at all times.

Rest is an important part of good health, and I get it when I can. But when my rodeo schedule's hectic my body doesn't have the luxury of a schedule. Sometimes I might drive all night and sleep from 6 in the morning to 1 in the afternoon. Getting enough rest and good food to eat is especially tricky in the summertime, when I'm on the go most of the time. When I get run-down, I might not feel as strong or think quite as clearly. But I don't ever

use lack of sleep (or anything else, for that matter) as an excuse. I don't say, "I didn't ride my best today because I didn't get my eight hours." I guess I could, but with an attitude like that I wouldn't win much.

I remember when I first cracked out with Cody. I'd grown up eating breakfast when I woke up in the morning, like most people do. Then I jumped into the rat race. I learned real quick that if you're going to rodeo for a living you have to take what you can get when you can get it, and learn how to preserve yourself or you'll never last. If you take care of yourself today you have a lot better chance of being able to compete — and win — tomorrow.

When I'm not getting enough rest is when being in shape saves me. The average American eats at 7 a.m., noon and 6 p.m. every single day. There are times in July when I might not have a chance to eat or sleep at all for a day or two. But that's life — and that's rodeo.

Stretching is just as important before and after I ride as it is before and after I work out. It's one of the first things I start doing when I get to a rodeo, and one of the last things I do before I leave. I stretch before, throughout and after every rodeo. I also stretch on  my days

Stretching my hamstrings.
(Kendra Santos Photo)

Stretching my hip flexors.
(Kendra Santos Photo)

Stretching my groin.
(Kendra Santos Photo)

off. Stretching keeps me warm and loose, and helps prevent injuries. It also helps me maintain a high level of flexibility.

When I get to a rodeo, I start stretching slowly and gradually, and keep stretching until I get on. It wouldn't do any good to warm up and then sit around an hour before I ride and let my muscles cool down. I've found that it's even more important to really stretch my muscles in the wintertime, because the cold weather makes me tight.

Before the bareback riding I stretch my neck with slow, rolling circles in each direction. Then I make big, slow arm circles for my arms and shoulders, going faster as I get warmed up. Another thing I do for my arms and shoulders is grab the top rail of a fence and hang with one hand at a time.

I stretch to the point of a sweat, so my body's awake and ready for what's ahead. I go to the point of feeling it, but not to the point of pain.

The groins and hamstrings are two of the most important things to stretch because they're the muscles that get hurt the most often in rodeo. The groin is where all your strain is when you try to ride an animal, especially a bull. The hamstrings are what pull your legs back from the knee during bareback and bronc riding spur strokes.

To stretch my groins, I bend one knee to the side and outstretch the other, with my outstretched foot facing forward. Then I roll onto the inside of my foot. Another groin stretch I use starts with my toes turned out, and my feet wide apart (just beyond shoulder width). I put my hands on my ankles, my elbows on my knees, and, while pushing my knees outward, squat down with my butt.

For my hamstrings, I bend down and grab my ankles, and hold for the count of eight. Then I put a leg up on

the rail of a fence and bend forward at the waist. Another hamstring stretch I like takes a towel. I lay down on my back, stick one leg up in the air, and hold an end of the towel in each hand. With the towel running across my arch, I pull the towel toward my head, which stretches my hamstring muscles.

For my hips, I cross my legs with my feet at shoulder width and lean with my hips toward the front leg, leaning my body back toward the foot that's in back. Trunk rolls, where I bend at the waist and rotate in a circular motion, are good for loosening up my hips, back and sides.

I do my stretching in my athletic shorts, riding pants, boots and spurs, and I do the same stretches for all three events. But I do extra neck and shoulder stretches before the bareback riding, extra trunk rolls and hamstring stretches before the bronc riding and a lot of groin stretches for the bull riding, because those are the most stressed parts of the body in each event.

I stretch before the rodeo starts and while I'm getting ready for each event; while doing things like changing my spurs. I keep stretching throughout every performance, and again after the bull riding, which is as important as warming up. Light stretching after physical exertion releases the acid that makes you sore out of the muscles, and makes a big difference in how I feel the next day.

I have a lot of respect and appreciation for the Justin SportsMedicine Team. The Justin crew has been a great addition to rodeo and cowboy health in general, and has helped me learn everything from proper stretching and taping methods to specific tricks for rehabilitating my knees and shoulders. I listen to those guys.

20 CENTS A MILE

I learned more as a PRCA rookie than any other year of my life. I learned so much about my equipment, my body and myself that year. You could say I grew up. I was young and enthusiastic, and there was a huge world waiting for me. I had a lot to learn, but I had the best teachers in the business.

I got my PRCA permit when I turned 18, in October of 1987. A permit allows you to enter rodeos that accept permits until you win enough money to "fill" your permit and buy your card. I filled my PRCA permit at four rodeos, and I was on my way. I was a wide-eyed kid who was so excited I could hardly see straight. I was broke, but that wasn't about to put a damper on my dreams. After all those years of getting slammed, then getting up and trying my heart out again to get it right, it was time to see if I had it in me to ride for a living.

I placed in all three events at the first PRCA rodeo I entered on my card, in Dayton, Ohio. That was my ticket to ride at any rodeo in the world and ride against guys I'd only seen on TV. Life was great, and that had a lot to do with Cody (Lambert), who took me under his wing when I was an 18-year-old kid nobody'd ever heard of.

Cody had seen me around for several years and told me to give him a call when I got my permit filled, so I did. It was one of the best moves I ever made. When I started rodeoing full time for the first time with Cody in 1988, it was like a whole new world. Up until that point I'd just gotten in my truck and driven to rodeos within a five-hour radius of my house. Cody showed me what the big leagues are all about. All of a sudden I was entering rodeos in places like Cloverdale, British Columbia, and buying $600 plane tickets. We were staying at the Hilton and eating steak dinners. When we rented a car, it was a Town Car.

< *Autographs. (Tim Mantoani Photo)*

I'd left home with just enough money to get me through the first week, and was pretty sure that a week of traveling in style like that was going to break me. I was a little nervous about setting out with the big boys without any money, but figured it was my time to give it a shot. It was win or go home. Thank God it worked out. But it was close, at first.

There were times we'd load up with Lane (Frost), Tuff (Hedeman) and Jim (Sharp), and go to a steakhouse and play a numbers game for who had to buy dinner. They'd ask me if I was in and I was so scared because I knew if I lost it would break me. But I was always in. I didn't want those guys to know I was afraid of anything.

At that time in my life I couldn't get to enough rodeos, and going from one to the next suited me just fine. When I was growing up, I dreamed of going to a rodeo every day. But I always had to go home to get back to school. Time went so slowly then, because I couldn't wait for the next weekend — the next rodeo — to roll around. When I joined the PRCA and could go to as many rodeos as I wanted, I loved that so much that I wanted time to slow down.

Throughout the years I traveled with Cody, he always wanted to go home to see his family — his wife, Leanne, and little boy, Riley. In the beginning, I remember asking him, "Do you hate rodeo?" I couldn't understand it. I wondered how he got to be such a great, famous cowboy feeling like that. But it didn't take long. By 1990, when I got my first place in Stephenville, I got excited about being home again, too. I built the fences around it myself and took pride in it. My horses and my dog were there. I finally understood the magnet that'd been pulling at Cody, and had a little more sympathy for his feelings.

When I showed up on the scene, Cody was traveling with Lane, Tuff and Jim. Four guys can "buddy" together and basically enter as a group using the same preferences. After I came along, Cody and I buddied together, and Lane, Tuff, Jim and, later, Clint Branger buddied together. But we all asked for the same preferences, so we traveled together a lot the first couple years of my career.

As a rookie, I was an easy target for their practical jokes. Their favorite prank was to trick me into doing all the driving. I'd start off behind the wheel. Then, at about 2 in the morning, one of them would take a turn. He'd drive for maybe 15 minutes, until they knew I was asleep. Then they'd turn the clock ahead to 5 a.m., pull over and act tired when they woke me up. A couple hours later, when it was supposedly 7 o'clock but it was still pitch black I'd figure out I'd been conned. Little did they know that, at that time in my career, I would have willingly driven all night to prove myself to them. I guess they didn't realize they were my heroes.

On one of those all-night drives, I remember turning the radio to a rock 'n' roll station. Cody said, "You don't like rock 'n' roll, do you?" "Oh, no," I told him. I might as well have said, "What kind of music do you like, Cody? From now on that's what I like, too."

I felt like I needed to prove to those guys that I belonged in their buddy group. I got on my first bull in front of Tuff and Cody one night at the Dos Amigos saloon and arena in Odessa, which is the same place I first hurt my left knee a few years later. I was trying so hard to impress them that a bull I could have ridden blindfolded threw me off. That embarrassed me and made me mad, so I got on a turnout bull, relaxed, went back to my original game plan and rode him. I stuck it on him, and learned another valuable lesson about trying the right way.

I was with winners from the get-go, and that rubs off on you. If you're traveling with guys who whine and make excuses, get out. That will do nothing but bring you down. I'm not saying you have to travel with world champions. You can go with your best friend as long as he has a positive attitude, and it works for you. The same goes for when you pick someone to help you behind the chutes. I always pick somebody I respect, because I want to get ready in a positive

Checking the handle of my bull rope with Cody. (David Jennings Photo)

atmosphere. Roach Hedeman helped me my first five years at the Finals. Then Lewis Field started helping me in 1994. Cody's helped me there, too, and so has Chad Klein. They're all winners with good attitudes, and they all know what they're doing.

Good attitudes were about the only thing my first group of traveling partners had in common. Their personalities were totally different, but they all knew how to win. Traveling with them felt like being a member of a wolfpack. We knew when we pulled into a rodeo that we weren't leaving without some money. Everyone else there knew it, too. That was quite a feeling for a rookie.

Cody — we call him "Klete," which is short for Kletus from the "Dukes of Hazzard" — has a really dry sense of humor. It takes people years and years to get to know him because he's so dry, and very few people ever know how to take him. He cracks jokes all day every day, and most people don't get them. He toys with guys who don't know him and they get real quiet, real fast. What's great about Cody is that he might never go back and tell them he was kidding.

It's hard to explain what Cody's really like. In the movie they made about Lane after he died, "Eight Seconds," they didn't even try to portray Cody like he really is. They cast him as a clever poet, which he's not, and didn't even attempt to tell it like it is. They really messed up there, because they missed out on a hell of a character. But then, like I said, it takes years to get to know Cody. And I'm not sure how they could have shown what he's really like in a two-hour movie.

Cody's so smart, but he's the kind of guy who loves for people who don't know him to think he's dumb. When he's making airline reservations is a perfect example. The agent will think he's just some stupid hillbilly cowboy. Then, before it's over, she'll be having a problem getting a reservation to work, and he'll rattle off exactly what she needs to do to get it done. He'll basically explain her job to her. Then the agent doesn't know what to think. Cody is really, really smart. But he talks slow, and that fools a lot of people into thinking he's simple. How many people do you know who try to act a lot smarter than they are? Cody's just the opposite.

Cody was the brains in the outfit, and handled a lot of the group's business, like entering and scheduling. But ever since we got to know each other really well, and got completely comfortable around each other, Cody and I have acted like two little kids. Dodge gives me a van to drive every year I win the all-around. One day early on in my career we decided we needed the van to be cool and dark in the daytime so one guy could sleep while the other guy drove. We had a brainstorm to spray paint the windows black. We could have taken it in to have the windows professionally tinted, but our way was more fun. We've done it that way in every one of my vans since.

Over the years, Cody and I became so close that we're like brothers. He's spent more time with me since we got together than he has with his wife. We can answer each other with a look. But in the beginning, I needed a mother hen to show me the ropes and keep me in line. I was the kid of the bunch, so I needed a lot of babysitting. Cody basically had to tell me when to go to bed, when to get up and when to pay for my share of the gas. It wasn't that I didn't think I should pay my share, I just didn't really think

about all those little details. I'd never been anywhere without my parents before. I was ready to ride in the PRCA, but didn't have much practice with all the other responsibilities that go along with it.

I didn't even have a credit card when I was a rookie, so we charged everything on Cody's cards. One day at Cheyenne that first summer, Cody walked up and asked me for $3,800. "For what?" I asked him. He explained to me that all that gas I'd pumped and those hotel beds I'd slept in weren't free. "OK," I said, and I opened up my little book where I kept track of my entry fees and where we'd been. I was happy to peel off rodeo checks and sign them over to him. I just kept peeling and signing until Cody told me to stop. Then Cody grabbed my book. He couldn't believe I'd been stuffing all my checks from the whole summer in there. I'd just figured I'd put them in the bank whenever we went home. After he'd counted up $50,000 worth of checks he handed my book back to me and just shook his head.

About that same time, I went through a spell of sleeping in. It was just typical teenager stuff. Cody told me one day that he was going to start waking me up one time in the morning. He was going to say, "Ty, get up" one time. If I didn't get up he was going to leave me. I was just a kid and I wasn't very worldly, so that scared me. I didn't want to wake up alone and stranded in some strange place. A few days later, I got knocked out in the bull riding at the rodeo in Salinas, California. Cody walked over and said, "Ty, get up," and I sat up right there in the arena, even though I wasn't actually conscious until awhile later out in the medics' tent.

All the attention I got when I was a PRCA rookie was kind of new to me. I remember riding a bareback horse at the rodeo in Window Rock, Arizona, and being mobbed by fans who wanted to talk to me and get my autograph. Without thinking, I did whatever they said. I guess I was so flattered that I forgot to stay focused on my reason for being there. I broke off all the fun just in time to go get on my bronc, but failed the fundamental lesson of business before pleasure. I was getting down on my bronc when Cody noticed I'd forgotten my spurs. He took his spurs off and put them on my boots real quick, right before I nodded. It was one of those embarrassing career moments I'd like to forget. But between Cody's unforgiving memory and my mom's video camera, I don't think it's going to happen in this lifetime.

There was another point in my rookie year when I was so sore I could hardly walk, much less ride, because one of my hamstring muscles was sore from my butt all the way down my leg. But I kept going because I didn't want Cody to see that I had a weakness. On the way to one rodeo he told me with a straight face about how he'd worn out a lot of little no-hearts like me. He never cracked a smile. After hearing that, I didn't plan to give up 'til I was dead. But Cody looked out for me in his own way. When we got to the rodeo he went and found my Uncle Butch (Myers) and had him talk me into going home to heal up.

When Cody and I branched off on our own more, in about 1990, we split the driving so it was dead even. If we had to drive 200 miles and he'd driven 101 miles I swear to God he'd back up a mile before turning the wheel over to me. Cody and I are both non-driving sons of guns. When other guys would catch rides with us we'd pay them to guarantee we didn't have to drive. We looked at it like insurance, and we were happy to give up $100 to avoid that wheel, because we hated it so much. In the end, we made a game out of seeing how much driving we could get out of.

One time I was driving, and Cody and Dave Appleton (the 1988 world champion all-around cowboy) were back sleeping on the bed in my van. It was about 2 in the morning, and I had the cruise control set at 85 miles an hour. I came up on a curve. I was really tired, and hadn't seen any warning signs, so I didn't think it was any big deal. I kept the cruise control on and started to make the turn. Pretty soon I was white-knuckling the steering wheel, and the tires were squealing. When the road finally started to straighten out I looked in my rear-view mirror. Those guys had popped their heads up, but as soon as they realized we weren't going to die they dropped back down real fast so I wouldn't catch them awake and ask them to drive. We didn't have a lot of sympathy for the other guy when he got tired, so you just had to buck up and go on.

One year, Cody and I flew early the morning of the Fourth of July out of Portland and into the Dallas-Fort Worth airport. We got to DFW early enough to where we could have driven to our destination, which was Pecos, Texas, in time for the rodeo that night. But we already had plane tickets to Odessa, which is near Pecos, so we figured we might as well get closer by plane and stay off the road. We boarded the plane and sat on the runway for two hours before the airline admitted defeat and let us get off because of some mechanical failure. But by then it was too late to drive it.

We found one charter service at DFW that was open on the Fourth, but it was going to cost us $3,000 to get 300 miles. Cody had a good bull and bronc drawn, so his decision was made. He had to go. I, on the other hand, had three dinks drawn. But you never know when an animal might wake up in the mood to buck, and I'd made it that far, so I wasn't about to bail on Cody.

Not long into our outrageously expensive flight, we realized our pilot was incompetent. Cody saw Pecos out the window and pointed it out to the guy, but he waited awhile before admitting he was lost and turning around. We'd called ahead and had a car waiting at the little airport in Pecos, so when we got there we pealed out for the rodeo grounds. When we squealed into the rodeo, my bareback horse was the last horse left in the chutes.

The clowns told a joke to buy me a couple minutes, and while I threw on my chaps and spurs, Cody put my riggin' on my horse. My saddle bronc and bull were true to

129

form and didn't buck. But my bareback horse had a good day for him and I placed on him. Cody won the saddle bronc riding and second in the bull riding, so we got out of there alive physically and financially.

We had a plane chartered another time and while we were flying the nose fell off of the prop. The old brush pilot we'd hired said it was no big deal, but we made him land it and got out and drove the rest of the way. I remember another pilot checking the gas tank with a lit cigarette hanging out of his mouth. Cody about broke his neck jumping out of that plane. We didn't mind taking a few risks along the way, and no one ever accused us of being chicken. But we aren't stupid, either.

I wasn't real impressive the first time I met Lane. I didn't know it at the time, but

Jim and I on the Sling Shot ride in Calgary. He told me he wasn't scared, but the sweat rings under his arms tell the real story. (Murray Family photo)

he always stayed awake and talked to you if he didn't know you. Taking the time to ask you about every detail of your life was his way of getting to know everyone really well. When he was traveling with someone for the first time, it was a guarantee that he'd stay up all night and drive so he could talk to that person. He was genuinely interested in finding out everything about everybody.

We left Denver one night, and Cody drove first. Then he woke me up to drive, so Lane jumped up and drove so he could talk to me. I played into his hand for a while, and rode on the passenger's side of Cody's truck and visited with him while Tuff and Cody slept in the back. I was still just a kid then, and I was worthless when I got tired. I had a habit of answering every question with "I don't know" when I was having trouble keeping my eyes open.

I enjoyed visiting with Lane, but within about 30 miles I was starting to nod off, so I climbed in back and went to sleep. Cody asked Lane the next morning why he didn't make me drive. Lane said, "That lazy son of a bitch, I asked him three or four questions and all he could say was 'I don't know.' He was too lazy to answer my questions, so I told him to go to sleep."

Everybody loved Lane. He had it all. He was kind of like Elvis, and everyone wanted to know him. But not everyone got to know the real Lane. He was a great guy, but he was a character, too. Right after I met him, early in my rookie year, we were sharing a hotel room. We flipped a coin for bed partners, and I was sharing a bed with Lane. He was somebody I really looked up to. He was a superstar when I was still in high school. To then become friends with him — as a rookie — was really something. We got in bed and he asked me if I'd ever seen his toenails. He told me they glowed in the dark. I was young and naive, so I looked under the covers. As soon as I got my head under there he farted. He thought that was really funny. Lane had a way of laughing at life, and sooner or later we all learned to laugh with him.

When one of us got drilled, Lane would slap his leg and laugh at us while we were staggering out of the arena. It was his way of reminding us that making a mistake in the arena wasn't the end of the world. That was Lane. He got some really big points across to me by smiling and laughing. Before I met Lane I'd feel my head turning red when I'd get bucked off because I felt like I'd just struck out or missed a pass. After that, I learned from my mistakes, then moved on.

When Lane got bucked off, on the other hand, he got mad. The rest of us used to love to see him get bucked off

130

when we had an all-night drive ahead of us, because he'd drive all night to punish himself. He wouldn't say a word, and when we got to the van he'd have it running, and be waiting on us for a change. Then, when we got there the next day, he was over it.

We had to drive all night from Salinas to Cheyenne in 1988, and Lane was driving because he'd gotten bucked off at Salinas and was mad. Jim, Tuff and Cody were on the bed. I was the rookie, so I was laying on the riggin' bags trying to sleep. We were getting close to Salt Lake City, where the salt water comes up to the side of the road. It was early in the morning, and the sun was just starting to come up. Lane spotted a huge carp in water that was too shallow. It was stranded, and couldn't swim. He pulled over

to the side of the road and got out, but the rest of us were so tired we kept sleeping.

Lane caught the fish, brought him over to the van and opened the door real quietly. He put that carp's mouth on my lips to give me a kiss, and woke me up with his smooching noises and laughing. Carp are the grossest fish there are. No one even eats them because they're so bony and greasy. They're really ugly, and they eat scum. They're like the buzzards of the water.

Lane enjoyed life. He made the most of every day. He was a great guy, and he went out of his way to make other people happy. Back in those days, that wasn't at the top of Tuff's priority list. He told it like it was, like it or not, and was a little rougher around the edges.

Mike Cason, me, Tuff Hedeman, Jim Sharp, Larry Williams and Lane Frost (in the front) at a 1988 bull riding in Dodge City, Kansas. (Photo courtesy of Ty Murray)

Lane and Tuff were best friends. But they were as opposite as two people can be. Everybody loved Lane, and he genuinely cared about everyone he met. We waited on Lane everywhere we went (unless, of course, he got bucked off). We'd be in a hurry trying to get to the next rodeo and would politely explain to fans that we were running late

performances a day. I couldn't get enough of riding then, so I got out there every performance and mounted out bucking horses and bulls that other guys had turned out. Stock contractors paid us $10 a head to mount out stock then, which basically amounts to an exhibition ride that doesn't count for the rodeo. I obviously didn't do it for the

Me and Klete, the kid and the veteran. (Sue Rosoff Photo)

and didn't want to have to turn out at the next one. We'd all load up in the truck or van, ready to blow out of there. But we couldn't leave, because Lane was over signing autographs, visiting and bouncing babies on his knee. He didn't just say hello and move along. He had in-depth conversations with people. He had a movie-star personality, and people went crazy over it.

I met Tuff in the fall of 1987, when I was still riding on my PRCA permit. We were at the rodeo in Kansas City. We were there for several days, and there were two

money, but I craved riding so much that I did everything I could think of to get better at it.

One day, I mounted out a bull that Cody's brother Casey had turned out. He was a fighting bull, and had no business being in the draw in the first place, but I figured you never know when you might draw a bull like that, so why not get the experience? Luckily, I survived.

I was there in Kansas City with a guy by the name of Todd Watkins. Cody was there with Tuff. From there, we were all headed to a bull riding in Abilene, so I asked

Cody if I could ride with Tuff. Cody said, "Sure," and jumped in with Todd. I took off with Tuff, and was pretty impressed to be in the same truck with him. We drove a long way like that, then Cody got back in with Tuff and they detoured off to Cody's in-laws' house. When I got back in with Todd I hadn't gotten any sleep, because I'd stayed up drinking coffee and talking to Tuff the whole way. Sure enough, I fell asleep at the wheel. When Todd woke up, we were flying through the air in his truck, headed into a ditch. I made Todd promise not to tell Cody, because he'd warned me to get some rest when Tuff was driving and I didn't feel like listening to another "How many times do I have to tell you?" lecture.

Tuff is tough. He always laughed at Lane for acting like a politician. Tuff drives like a maniac, and always has. One year, when Lane had a new van, he and his wife, Kellie, were waiting on the side of the road to hook up with Tuff and drive to a rodeo. Tuff came screeching down the road, and drove into the gravel where Lane was parked to slide up next to him. He kept sliding, and cratered right into the side of Lane's brand new van. Tuff stepped out and said, "Sorry," jumped into the van and off they went. If Lane had done that to Tuff he'd have felt terrible. He'd have apologized all over himself and taken it to get fixed.

We were traveling in Cody's truck another time and Tuff drove it under a tree and tore a big hole in the roof of the camper. He stopped, got out and asked Cody, "Got insurance?" That's Tuff, and you've got to love him.

I remember another time when Tuff, Jim and I were driving to a rodeo in Louisiana. Lane wasn't with us, but we'd borrowed that brand-new van. It was a really plush extended van with a fancy paint job. The dealer gave it to Lane as a sponsorship deal, and painted "World Champion Bull Rider Lane Frost rodeos with a so-and-so kind of van" on the side of it. It was pouring down rain and we were running late.

Tuff, who drives like a wreck looking for a place to happen, was driving when we came up on a "Detour" sign. Tuff said we didn't have time for a detour, so he punched it and drove right around that sign. All of a sudden, the pavement ended. Construction crews had torn out all the asphalt and were making a new pad and widening the road. It was just dirt at that point, and with 10 inches of rain on it was more like mush. It was solid slop for several miles. Of course Tuff hit it going about 90, so we were sideways in it. He had to keep the accelerator pushed to the floor the entire way to get through it.

There were times we were only going five miles an hour, but he had it floored just to keep making forward progress. We'd go sideways in one direction for a while, then we'd go sideways the other way awhile. We finally made it to the rodeo. Tuff got us there right on time. Then Lane showed up. He'd flown in to meet us. His fancy brand new van looked like a giant dirt clod, but he just laughed.

Jim cracks me up, but he doesn't say much. He's definitely the shy, quiet type, unless you're one of his best friends. Once you get to know him he says what he thinks, just like Tuff. That's a great trait, in my eyes. Tuff and Jim are as great as there's ever been in the bull riding. And Jim's the coolest under pressure. When he'd ridden his first nine bulls at the 1988 NFR and no one had ever ridden all 10 bulls, there were 18,000 people in that building who were worried about him riding that 10th one — everyone but Jim. And he's the same guy every day, everywhere.

That's a good thing about 95 percent of the time. I remember once when a bareback horse fell with me at the rodeo in Oklahoma City and knocked me out. Jim and Tuff were sitting on the back of the chutes, watching and waiting for the bull riding. When I came to, all I could hear was those two yelling, "Get the hell out of the arena — you're holding up the rodeo!" It's pretty hard to sit around feeling sorry for yourself with support like that from the people closest to you.

133

Cody, Jim and Tuff are my best friends and my heroes. I'll never forget Lane, either. I owe so much to all of them. I respect them more than I can say, and they've had a huge impact on my career and my life. We've been broke down and stranded every way possible, and have eaten at dives where there was no possible way a human was supposed to consume the food and survive. We've been to hell and back five or six times, and I wouldn't trade it for a million bucks. Of course, a million dollars in rodeo is a relative thing. Just because you've won a million dollars doesn't mean you're a millionaire. I crossed the million-dollar mark in career earnings over the Fourth of July run in 1993 (and became the youngest cowboy millionaire ever at 23) on the way to my fifth world all-around championship. I'll never forget what Lewis Field told me about winning a million dollars in rodeo: "It works out to about 20 cents a mile."

The Texas Cowboy Hall of Fame in Hico. (Kendra Santos Photo)

I remember saying early on in my professional career that I'd ride for nothing. That's how much I love what I do. In reality, I guess I couldn't really do that or I'd starve to death. But riding great animals is more fun to me than anything else on earth. I got started riding calves in the back yard for nothing, and there was no crowd to impress except my parents and my sisters. My love for riding is what's carried me all the way through. Money and fame were never the ultimate goal.

I can honestly say that I've never thought to myself, "All right! I won a big check. Next time I'm going to try to win an even bigger one." If money was my motivator I could think of 10,000 much safer and more profitable business ventures than rodeo.

Great rides are what make me happy. One ride that really sticks out from the 1990 NFR was my bareback ride on Bernis Johnson's Sippin' Velvet. He's the greatest bareback horse to ever draw a breath of air, in my opinion, because he bucked the hardest. He was the rankest, and he bucked hard the entire eight seconds. He got more guys on the ground than any other horse, and he threw off every great bareback rider that rode during his career.

Harry Vold's Bobby Joe Skoal has been a great horse, too. If you make a good ride on him it's for all the chips. I've had him five times and won five rodeos on him. In 1993, I had him at Fort Smith, Arkansas; Colorado Springs, Colorado; Dodge City, Kansas; and Cheyenne, Wyoming. People started accusing me of cheating because I was drawing him so much. You know you've got a great one when you see dollar signs when your name shows up next to his on the draw sheet. That's Bobby Joe. Every bronc rider who can really ride licks his chops over drawing him.

Dan Russell's Skoal's Pacific Bell is the best bull of all time, in my opinion. He didn't have a pattern; he did whatever it took to get you on the ground. He'd leap six feet in the air sideways and turn back. Pacific Bell had strength, speed, horns and muscle; he was mean and he

My sponsor CLS Transportation makes my life a lot easier with all the traveling I do. (Kendra Santos Photos)

I had the opportunity to drive a racecar during the 1998 PBR Finals at the Las Vegas Motor Speedway. What a blast. (Kendra Santos Photo)

At the Stephenville Walk of Fame ceremony in 1998. (Dudley Barker Photo)

The Murray Gang — my sisters, Kerri and Kim, me, my mom and dad, Butch and Joy. (Kendra Santos Photo)

was smart. There were times I watched that bull buck and it made me shudder. I wondered if there was a human alive who could ride him on those days.

I have a lot of favorite rides that I've made and they're not all famous, high-point rides. I never judge a ride by the points or the money. I like the ones where I have to bear down and try harder every jump. That's what rodeo's all about.

I have as much respect for rodeo's great animal athletes as I do for great cowboys. To be the best at anything is a big accomplishment. I feel the same way about the great stock contractors. They know so much about every aspect of this sport, from having an eye for great bulls and broncs to running a rodeo without a hitch. Guys like Fred Dorenkamp are the masters, in my mind, because they've seen so many generations of cowboys come and go.

Earning their respect is a big deal to me, because they've seen it all. They know all about the mud, the blood and

the beer. When you're cowboying up in the chute on a trashy bronc, they notice that and they appreciate it. They see things most other people don't, and can teach you so much if you listen and pay attention. I learned early that if you keep your eyes open and your mouth shut when you're learning about this sport you'll have a lot better chance of getting somewhere. Guys like Fred and Harry (Vold) have been down the road I'm headed four or five times already, so I like to watch them work.

I have a ton of respect for guys like (16-time World Champion Cowboy) Jim Shoulders, too. So being complimented by someone like him means everything to me. I worked my whole life to try to be equally exceptional in all three events. To do that — and then have Jim Shoulders tell me he can't find a weakness and can't pick which event I do best — that's as good as it gets for me.

It's also a hell of a compliment to be loved by so many fans — especially considering that they've cheered for me and pulled for me so many years. To know that there are people who've never given up on me, not even when I was hurt, is amazing to me.

Having people pull for me makes a big difference when I ride, because the home-field advantage is a proven fact. Athletes do better when thousands of people are cheering for them, and are rallied behind them in their corner. When I'm about bucked off and hear 20,000 people screaming their lungs out for me, it gives me that extra I need to hang on.

I don't usually hear *what* an announcer's saying when I'm getting on — before the gate cracks — because I'm in my own world. And I don't usually hear *what* the fans are screaming when I'm hanging on by my fingertips with pure determination. But I do hear them, and I know it makes me try just a little harder because they're behind me.

I learned to respect and appreciate rodeo fans early in my career. It's easy to be a jerk when you get tired and a lot of people start making a bunch of demands on your time. But I saw it happen to other people, and I vowed not to let it happen to me. I feel like anytime anybody thinks enough of me to want my autograph, that ought to flatter me enough to take the time to give it to them. If someone thinks enough of me to walk over to me, out of their way, and wait in line to get my autograph, I'm going to take the time to meet them and find out where they're from and something about them. If the table was turned, I'd expect them to do the same.

I'll always remember how I felt when I was a little kid. I looked up to guys like Donnie Gay, Larry Mahan and Denny Flynn. As far as I was concerned, no one in the world was greater or more famous than those guys. They were the guys who took a little extra of their time and gave it to kids like me. You can't believe what that did for me. It made my whole year. So I figure the extra time it takes to be good to people is worth whatever effort it takes. Lane felt that way. That's why he had such a great career and life, and part of what made him so special.

It flatters me that little kids look up to me now. But I don't try to put up any fronts or act according to any certain image. I'm just me. It'd be too hard to go around faking to be somebody I'm not all the time. And I think if kids are going to learn something by watching me, that's an important thing to learn. The people I admire and respect most in this world are that way. They don't change no matter what — no matter where they are or who's around, they're always the same people. It doesn't matter if you're the president or a hay farmer, they're going to treat you the same. I love that.

The basic rules of the rodeo game go like this: Roughstock cowboys are allowed to count their earnings from 125 rodeos toward qualifying for the National Finals Rodeo and winning world championships. Timed-event contestants and all-around contenders can count 100 rodeos toward world titles. The basic philosophy is that it's harder for timed-event guys to get to as many rodeos because they have to haul horses and can't fly as much. So, to make it fair between the two ends of the arena in the all-around race, only 100 rodeos count.

The PROCOM staff assumes you want to enter a rodeo as "official," or count it toward the world standings, unless you tell them otherwise. Once you reach your rodeo limit, the PRCA automatically stops counting your earnings toward the world standings or NFR qualification.

In the roughstock events, there's an exception to the official rodeo rule. If you draw up in slack, when stock contractors are notorious for bucking their dinks because there aren't any fans in the stands, that rodeo is assumed "unofficial" and doesn't count unless you notify PROCOM otherwise. When you unofficial a rodeo you get paid if you win, just like usual. But if you do win something it doesn't count toward the world standings.

Me and my best buddy Jim discussing our rides at a PBR Bud Light Cup event. (Gary Jensen Photo)

There are a few guys every year, usually rookies, who miscalculate their official rodeo count and run out of rodeos before the end of the season. In other words, they burn up all their rodeos and can't count anything they win at the last few big ones toward the standings. It's a tough lesson learned, but just one of many in this sport.

I don't have to worry about that, because when I'm rodeoing I only enter about half the rodeos I'm allowed. I personally like a 60-rodeo-a-year season for every reason. I stay fresher and crave it more when I'm not driving all night day in and day out, and rodeoing myself into the ground. It lets me get home to enjoy my ranch, and to spend some time with my family and friends. That's really important to me. The bottom line's better that way, too, because I spend a lot less money on entry fees and travel expenses. In my opinion, the main thing is to get to enough rodeos to get to the Finals, because that's where all the money's made.

I also go to all the PBR Bud Light Cup Tour events, and a few of PBR's U.S. Smokeless Tobacco Co. Touring Pro Division events. I was a founding shareholder of the cowboy owned and operated organization, and am so proud of how far we've come since having our first full season in 1994. Twenty of us plunked down $1,000 apiece just a few short years ago. We took a chance on our belief that the combination of the very best bull riders and bulls in the world could make it as a stand-alone sport, and we've hit a home run. The 1994 PBR Tour was worth a then-impressive $250,000. The 2001 Tour was worth $7.2 million, and was capped off by the $1.75 million PBR Bud Light Cup World Championships in Las Vegas. That's what I call progress.

PBR's the best thing to happen to cowboys in a long time. It's great for everyone else involved, too, from the fans to the sponsors. I'm not cussing rodeo. I've loved this sport my whole life, and all my dreams have always revolved around it. I'm sure rodeo will be a big part of my life my whole life. I just hope it'll follow PBR's lead and strive for some serious progress. I think we need to concentrate on building a tour of really good rodeos for the very best contestants.

No other professional sport allows anyone who feels like it to walk onto the field whenever they want. The "Everybody Plays" approach is great for Little League, but this is the Majors. The best stock should not be wasted on someone who rodeos for a hobby and has no chance. The guys who ride the best should get paid the most, and the fans who buy the tickets should get the professional show they pay for. That seems so fair and obvious, but it's often not the case because of situations when the guys who ride for a living draw the dinks and the part-timers draw the rank ones they can't possibly ride.

The truth is, there are leagues of cowboys just like there are leagues of football and baseball players, and separating those leagues would be to everyone's advantage. Guys at the upper end of the lower-caliber leagues would have a chance to be stars at their level, and the very top level would be true professional rodeo. Thanks to the PBR, I know it's possible. It's not likely that rodeo will get that far during my career, but I hope to see it in my lifetime.

There's so much more to rodeoing for a living than just showing up to ride. And if you don't handle all the business that goes with it you'll never make it, I don't care how well you ride. Cody's the king at entering rodeos. He's studied it and understands the system better than anyone else. He's handled all my entering since I started rodeoing in the PRCA, and has continued to take care of that end of my career since he retired at the end of 1996. (Lambert started riding broncs part time, and winning, again in 1999.)

It's been such a huge advantage for me to have a guy like Cody on my side from the start. I remember wanting to enter El Paso, Texas, and Arcadia, Florida, my first year. But Cody knew we couldn't make it work because we had to ride two head in each event at El Paso. It wasn't possible to make both rodeos. When you're a rookie, you don't even know whether or not Bonifay, Florida has an airport. But Cody did. Just being with someone who knows where the rodeo arena is when you blow into town during the grand entry is a big advantage.

The first thing Cody looks at when making the decision on which rodeos to enter is the added money. That's the main factor because, we always figured, even if it's your favorite town or your hometown, we want to ride at the rodeo that pays the most money. If the money's equal at two rodeos and I can't make both of them, we look at the stock contractors involved and which rodeo will have the best stock. What we're trying to figure out is where my odds of drawing a bull or bronc I can win on are the best. We also try to avoid rodeos with stock contractors that only have one or two stars in their herd because my odds of drawing them aren't very good.

The stock is so important, because if the competitive opportunity isn't there, there's no point in walking across the street for a rodeo. When the stock's sorry, anyone can win because there's so much luck involved. If the guys who can really ride get the dinks, they have no chance. The best guys win when the bulls and broncs buck. That's when it comes down to talent.

Then we consider where I'll be when I need to go to each rodeo, and what it'll take to get there. Maybe a simple flight or drive will do it. But is it still a good idea if it'll take a commercial flight, a charter flight and a rental car to get there? We also factor in where I'll be heading after the rodeo in question, and whether or not it fits into an extended itinerary that makes sense.

Once we decide to enter me in a rodeo, we talk about which performance to ask for when Cody calls PROCOM. That's called a "preference." You get to give a first preference and a second preference. Then, everyone who enters the rodeo is randomly drawn a priority number by a computer. Basically, the guys who draw a high position on the priority list get their first preferences, the guys down in the middle might get their second preferences, and the guys at the bottom fill in the blanks by taking the spots no one else wanted.

Entering me is a challenge because I work more than one event. That's why I'm so thankful to have Cody on the case. He weighs out all the factors, like when each stock contractor bucks his best ones. You want to be up on Saturday night at a Harry Vold rodeo, for example, because that's when his very best buckers are out. My first preference considers the stock and the perfect combination of rodeos that avoid repeat trips back to the same rodeo.

For me, Plan B usually means asking for the performance no one else wants. Cody enters me as soon as entries open to make sure I get in. Then he waits until the entries are about to close and calls PROCOM back to find out when no one else wants to be up. When I ask to be up then I have a much better shot at getting up in all three events at the same time and avoiding an extra trip or two

to work my three events. Getting split up by events is a bad deal because it often leads to turnouts. And I hate to turn out. But working three events gives me three times the chance of drawing up at two rodeos the same day and being forced to turn out at one of them. So while I might forgo the best pen of bulls and broncs by requesting the preference no one else wants, at least I can ride everything in one performance and get on to the next rodeo.

Thirty minutes after entries close for a rodeo, you can draw out or change your preference. As you've probably figured out by now, you can get tied to a phone pretty fast in rodeo. Cody says the best job he ever did entering me was in 1994, when his leg was hurt and he sat in his office all day planning my schedule and making calls. Staying on top of the business side of rodeo — the entering and travel-agent type work — is a full-time job in itself when you take it as seriously as Cody does. But it makes a huge difference in how your year goes.

When I do draw up at a rodeo on a day that's impossible to fit into my schedule, I can trade positions with someone else if I can find someone willing to trade with me. Until 1997, we could only trade in the second round or later. Trading in the first round or at one-headers wasn't allowed. That rule's been changed, under the condition that our conflict is with another PRCA rodeo. If the conflict is with another organization, including PBR events, trading isn't allowed.

To get traded, I need to find someone who drew up when I want to go and ask him to trade spots. If I can't find anyone at the rodeos in person who might consider trading, Cody or I have to track people down by phone. Sometimes it takes several calls to find someone who'll do it, and other times we can't find anyone who'll do it and I have to turn out. When we do find someone who'll trade with me, there's paperwork to fill out in the rodeo secretary's office that makes the trade official. Trades can also be handled by phone through PROCOM. Both guys have to call in and say it's OK to make the switch, and we have to get it taken care of before the stock's drawn. They do that because no one would trade with you if they knew they had a good one drawn and you had a dink. Stock's randomly drawn by a computer, just like positions, by the way.

Turning out makes me sick, because it's a wasted opportunity. But when I can't find anyone who'll trade with me and am drawn up at two or more rodeos at the same time I have to turn out. I never turn out just because I don't like the bulls or broncs I've drawn, because you never know when they might wake up one morning and decide to buck. One year at Nampa, Idaho, I got Mike Cervi's bronc Needles for a reride. Needles was a notorious dink, and he'd been turned out all year because of it. But I went ahead and got on him, because I was there. I was 86 points on him, and won the rodeo. Another NFR bronc rider, Kyle Wemple, drew Needles, too. He would've turned him out, but he heard I was 86 on him, so he made the trip. He was 84 on him and won second. I've won on the dinks and had the great ones run off with me. You never know.

I have noticed that eight seconds flies when you're tapped off with a great animal. When you're on a scattering, belly-rolling pig that's hard to ride — one that jars your guts but you can't be any points on him — eight seconds can feel like forever. It's kind of like winning and losing that way, I guess. It's that old "Time flies when you're having fun" deal.

Turning out's no good for the committees, either, who've told the people in their town who's going to ride when. When fans show up and buy a ticket based on that information and then the plan falls through, they tend to get disappointed. I can't blame them for that, and hope the system will be improved sometime soon.

When I do have to turn out, I have to notify PROCOM at least three hours before the performance I'll be missing in order for that turnout to be considered "notified." Then it only costs me my fees and, in the bareback and saddle bronc riding, the amount of money the stock contractor pays someone else to mount out the horse I turned out in order

to fill the performance. Non-notified turnouts cost you your fees, the mount-out charge and a $50 fine. And if you're late sending your fees and fine into PROCOM, you get another fine. It's pretty easy to see the importance of taking care of business in this sport. If you don't, it'll cost you.

I've never tried drugs — not even a puff of pot. But I will drink a beer with you every now and then, after I'm done riding or a long day of work at the ranch. I don't remember much about the last time I got really drunk, but it left enough of an impression on me that I might never do it again. In 1994, the top 12 bull riders in the United States were invited to Barretos, Sao Paulo, Brazil for an international competition between the U.S., Brazil and Australia. The Festa do Peao de Boiadeiro lasted four days, and 80,000 people were there to see each performance. It was a pretty amazing event. A lot of people don't realize that rodeo is second only to soccer in Brazil, and the people there treat rodeos like a big party.

The night before I was supposed to ride the best bull in Brazil, the owner of the bull handed me a shot of a clear drink to toast the match. Big bucks were bet on the ride, but it seemed to me like an innocent enough "may-the-best-man-win" gesture, so I accepted the toast and swallowed the shot. In about two minutes it about dropped me. We'd heard stories about a drink called Pinga that can make you deaf and blind, but I didn't dream that that friendly stock contractor would try to kill me off with it. I puked and then passed out.

When I woke up, I wandered out into the streets looking for a little fresh air and our bus to take me back to where we were staying. I ended up getting lost in the street, but a couple of Brazilians found me puking on the sidewalk. The only English words they knew were, "Take easy." I was trying to draw them a picture of a bus and show them where I wanted

A great bull in Brazil that was previously unridden. Tens of thousands of dollars were bet on this ride. I was in the 90s on him after he turned back both ways. (Armindo Almeida photo)

to go with my hands, but they didn't understand. They picked me up and carried me to a hospital, which was right on that street. Next thing I knew a doctor walked in with a bottle of medicine, a needle and a syringe. I jumped up, and the two Brazilians tried to hold me down.

I felt like I was in "The Twilight Zone." My eyesight was hit-and-miss — blurry then clear — but I couldn't believe that was happening to me. I slung the Brazilians off of me and ran back out on the street, where I nearly got hit by a bus. The bad news was I about died right there on that street. Two seconds later and I'd still be splattered all over the Brazilian blacktop. The good news was that the bus missed me, and the other American bull riders were on it.

One of them picked me up and put me in the bus, and that's the last thing I remember. I passed out for the night.

We were staying in a monastery, and they carried me to bed. Daryl Mills, who won the PRCA world bull riding championship that year, filled my ears with green toothpaste. When my dad walked in the next morning and started talking to me I couldn't hear him. It scared me for a minute, but by then I was putting 2 and 2 together, and 4 equaled Pinga. The stock contractors bet tens of thousands of dollars on that ride. I was the sickest guy in the world when I got on that bull that night, but I got the guy back by riding his prized bull. He was a great bull. He kicked straight up in the air and spun both ways. He was a bull you could've won a round on at the NFR. It was my idea of fun, even with a headache and a queasy stomach. The moral of the story for me, when it comes to experimenting with drugs and other foreign substances, is "Just say no."

THE SHOW

I still wore Pampers under my Wranglers when I started my riding career at age 2. But in my mind I wasn't riding cute little calves in front of my parents and sisters in that run-down old arena in our back yard. I was twisting fire-breathing eliminators at the National Finals Rodeo, and 20,000 fans were screaming their lungs out for me.

There's not another feeling in the world like walking down the tunnel that leads from the contestant locker rooms to the arena at the NFR. When you get to the end of that tunnel and 15 of the greatest, most talented animals on the face of the earth are staring you down, hard as rocks, snorting and spooking, it makes the hair stand up on the back of your neck. When you make eye contact with the likes of High Chaparral, Bodacious and Gunslinger, it can do one of two things to you. It can either scare the hell out of you, or it can stop you in your tracks and make you say to yourself, "This is it. This is why I do this."

The NFR is The Show; the big time; the epitome of the sport. It's what you live for when you're a professional cowboy, and is the true test of who the most determined and willing cowboy is. The NFR is rodeo's ultimate showcase event, and is one of the greatest sporting events in the world. It's not the $4-million-plus payoff, standing-room-only crowds, top contestants and livestock that make the NFR so spectacular — it's a combination of all of it.

The top 15 contestants in each event, based on money won during the regular (November-to-November) season, qualify for the NFR in December, which since 1985 has been held at the Thomas and Mack Center in Las Vegas. World championships are won and lost at the Finals, and if anyone who rodeos for a living tells you he doesn't want to win a world championship

< Just won my sixth World All-Around Championship at the 1994 NFR. (Dan Hubbell photo)

he's lying to you. A lot of times, when it's 3 o'clock in the morning and you're driving down the road and you're so tired you can barely keep your eyes open, if you think about winning a championship you can keep driving. I think about it every day of the year. If that sounds like an exaggeration to you, remember that guys like me didn't play tag in the back yard when we were kids; we played rodeo.

The NFR is what pays the bills and determines a cowboy's profit margin for the year. The fact that some cowboys bank an entire year on the NFR adds to the tension back behind the chutes. If a guy's been to 125 rodeos, qualifies for the Finals in the 15th hole and has a wife and kids at home, there's a good chance he's in the red. But the NFR payoff's so good these days that a lot of guys figure it's worth the risk and added pressure. Thanks to that big money, no lead is safe at the Finals anymore. If a guy gets hot there, it's possible to jump from 15th to first in those 10 days.

Handling the pressure at the Finals comes naturally to some contestants. Others have to fight it. But it's a key to success there. You can let the buzz of the press room, all the reporters' questions and speculations intimidate you, or you can feed off of it. The great cowboys rise to the occasion, and use the electricity in that building to take their game up a notch or two. They take that nervous energy and use it to be extra aggressive.

Every contestant at the Finals has a huge amount of respect for all of rodeo's animals. In a way they're our opponents in the roughstock events, but they're really more like our partners, because they're responsible for half of our scores. If they don't buck we don't win. The animals at the Finals earn the right to be there just like the contestants, over the course of an entire year. They've proven themselves to be consistently spectacular or they wouldn't be there.

The contestant directors set "pens" of animals at the Finals by category, which basically means they try to make the animals used in each round as even as possible so the

winner is determined by who rides best, and not who draws best. The cowboys have nicknames for which animals buck each night, like the "tweet pen," which are the bulls and broncs that are "nice" to ride; the "eliminator pen," which are the ones that are almost impossible to ride; and the "TV pen" or "rank pen," which are the very best buckers of all. The TV pen is the juice. That's why they always buck in the 10th round, when the world championships are on the line and the whole world's watching.

But at the NFR level it really doesn't matter what they run in the chute. Every animal there is a headliner in his own right, and deserves to be there. They're smart. They're great athletes. They're the best.

Finals fans are incredible, too, not just because they pack the place every night, but because they're knowledgeable. They're hard-core rodeo lovers who follow the sport all year long, and they plan their annual vacations around the Finals.

It's gotten really hard to get a ticket to the NFR over the years. The demand's a lot higher than the supply, so they sell out fast. But the toughest ticket there is the one that'll get you back behind the chutes. I don't think most people understand how hard it is just to get to the Finals, much less to do well once you get there. There's the mental strain, the physical strain and the financial strain.

Qualifying for the NFR requires complete dedication, and takes so much more than just riding good. And that doesn't change after you get there. The NFR is a whirlwind for all of us. Between the sponsor parties, charity events, photo sessions, press conferences, autograph signings, interviews and awards ceremonies, it's amazing a guy can find time to eat, sleep and ride.

I've always felt lucky to get to bed by 1 a.m. at the Finals, and that's never included dancing, drinking or partying. There isn't time for any of that. The closest thing to a party the cowboys attend is the go-round buckles ceremony after each performance. A cowboy's in his element

Pulling Cody's bull rope at the 1989 NFR. (Sue Rosoff Photo)

Getting ready to ride a bull at The Show. (PRCA Photo by Mark Reis)

at the arena for two hours a day during the performance. Ironically, that's the smallest part of his day.

After being named the 1988 PRCA/Resistol Overall and Bareback Riding Rookie of the Year, I qualified for my first National Finals Rodeo in 1989 and made the 15-cowboy cut in two events, the bareback riding and saddle bronc riding. I just missed making it in the bull riding. I ended up 19th in the final world bull riding standings that year, and that made me want it even more the next year. I turned 20 just before that first Finals. I went in sitting third in the world all-around standings behind two of my heroes, Clay O'Brien Cooper and my Uncle Butch. I'd actually won more than they had going into the Finals, but when the PRCA took away all my earnings after 100 rodeos I was third. Less than $7,000 separated the three of us. Clay made the Finals in the team roping that year, and Butch was there in the calf roping and steer wrestling.

I didn't go to the Finals that year thinking, "Hey, this is great. I made it to the National Finals in two events." It was more like, "This is great. I've been in the running all year long. Now let's go on with it." I knew by then that if I stuck with what got me that far I could have my world championship dream.

In the end, the 1989 all-around championship came down to Clay and I in the 10th round. I made two good rides on the horses I had. I did the best I could with what I'd drawn. So when I got off my bronc I waved my hat and put it back on. I didn't do that because I knew I'd won the world all-around championship, because at that time I didn't know the final outcome. I did it because, whether I won the world championship or not, I knew I'd done everything I could do. I had a feeling of contentment when I got off that last horse because I'd pulled out all the stops and given it everything I had.

As it turned out, the $58,031 I won at the Finals that year bumped my annual earnings up to $134,806, and was enough for my first world all-around championship by $17,317. That first gold buckle pounded in a point I'd always believed: If you really want something more than anything else — and you try as hard as you can — anybody can be a champion. The same principle explains why most people don't become champions. Everybody that rodeos says, "Yeah, I'd like to be a world champion." But just dreaming about it or saying you want it doesn't get it. You have to want it more than anything else in the world. You have to dedicate your life to it, think about it and work at it every day. I did that.

I remember walking into the Thomas and Mack Center building every night before the rodeo that first year and staring at a great big poster of the all-around buckle that was hanging in the concourse. Every day when I walked over to the elevator to go down to the locker room I looked at that buckle. Every day. That Sunday night, the first time I held that gold buckle in my hands, I couldn't take my eyes off of it. I was pretty numb when I stepped up on that stage to get it. I was kind of choked up, so my speech was pretty short. I remember thanking Lane, who'd died in July, Tuff, Cody and Jim for all their help and inspiration. I looked up to them as great champions then, and still do. All of us always believed that when we did good we could do better. When we did great we could do better. Even when we did something spectacular, we looked for a way to do even better than that.

I also thanked my family for all their sacrifices and support at that first PRCA World Champions Banquet. They worked toward that goal with me for the first 20 years of my life. When I look back at everything my parents did for me and my sisters when we were kids — the great life they gave us and how they always put us first — it amazes me.

People asked me that whole week if I was surprised by how well I was doing at such a young age; so early in my career. I reminded them that I didn't just wake up one day with a gold buckle on my belt. Becoming a world champion isn't something that sneaks up and surprises you. There's too much that goes into it. I had waited my whole life and tried so hard every day to get to that point. There was nothing sudden about it. It was a dream fulfilled, but I'd been climbing the ladder half a rung at a time since I was 2 to get there. When I won my first buckle when I was 5 it was a big deal. When I won the Arizona state championship in steer riding in the 9-12 age group it was an even bigger deal. Each success along the way was really important, and they kept getting bigger.

That first championship taught me that you can't flip the switch to cruise control and stay on top. The headlines said I was the cowboy king, but I still had to drive my share. I still had to stay in shape and keep striving to improve in every event. I still had to put my neck on the line every day. I knew the day I stopped paying that price would be the day the guy who wanted it worse than I did would kick my butt. I also knew I'd shake his hand, because he'd deserve to do it.

After winning $72,818 at the 1990 Finals, I won $213,722 and my second world all-around championship. It was the first time anyone had ever won more than $200,000 in a season, and I won the all-around by almost $100,000. But that wasn't the highlight for me. Getting to the Finals in all three events meant a lot more. After working so hard for so long to be equally strong in all three events, it was really gratifying to make the cut in all three. It wasn't because I was only the third guy ever to ride at the Finals in three events the same year (Bobby Berger did it in 1971 and Larry Mahan did it from 1966-70 and in 1973). I had tried my hardest and it paid off. When you're riding bucking horses and bulls, the crowds, the money and all the statistics are great. But if I can try my hardest every single time to make a better ride than I did the time before, I've got something.

149

On my way to my seventh world all-around championship at the 1998 NFR. (Dan Hubbell Photos)

Walking back to the chutes after a bronc ride at the 1994 NFR. (Dan Hubbell Photo)

I won $244,231 in 1991, including $101,242 at the Finals. Being there in three events with the lead I had gave me a pretty good chance of winning my third world all-around championship. But I knew not to stray from my usual one-ride-at-a-time game plan. It doesn't matter if I'm $2 ahead or $2 behind, way out front or way behind — none of that has anything to do with the task at hand, which is always the best ride I'm capable of.

an event title. Of course I wanted to do that. If I want to win on every single ride it only makes sense that I'd like to win world championships in every event, too. That's always something I shoot for. But throughout my professional career I have refused to single out one event and work harder at it or give it preferential treatment over the others. I never picked an event world championship to win. I try to win it all every time I ride in every event.

I was 85 points on Calgary Stampede's Zippy Delivery in the 10th round at the 1999 NFR. (Dan Hubbell Photo)

You hear guys say, "Stay in the average," (which at the NFR is won by the contestant with the highest total score in 10 rounds), especially at the Finals. I don't think that way. I try to win every go-round at every rodeo. If you can win every go-round, you will win the average. I go at the NFR like it's 10 rodeos, not to barely hang in there all week and see how I can end up in the average when it's over.

Around the time of that third world championship I started getting a lot of heat from the press about winning

I won $225,992 and my fourth world all-around championship in 1992. During the middle of the week at the Finals that year, a lot of the media people in the press room were quizzing me about, "What was wrong?" My old buddy Jim Sharp even left me a phone message at 3 o'clock the morning of the 10th round telling me he hadn't seen my name in the results much the last couple days. He was kidding, of course. Jim knows as well as I do that even Babe Ruth didn't hit it out of the park every time he took a swing. And I got out of town with $86,268, which doesn't sound like a bad week's work to me.

By the time 1993 rolled around I'd cut way back on my rodeo pace and was only going to about 60 rodeos. But, like I've said before, the main thing is getting to the Finals, and getting there in three events again was a big feather in my hat. I won my fifth world all-around championship that year, and my first event title in the bull riding. I also won the bareback riding average at the Finals which, in my opinion, is the second highest honor in rodeo next to a world championship.

I won $297,896 for the year, and only had half the expenses and half the wear-and-tear on my body as I would have if I'd gone to 120 rodeos. I'm no mathematician, but entering the best rodeos, getting on the best stock and riding for the biggest money made sense to me. Besides, 60 rodeos isn't exactly a walk in the park when you're talking about riding in three events. That's as many rides as a one-event guy would make at 180 rodeos.

I won the 1993 world bull riding championship by $95 over Canadian Daryl Mills, who won the 1994 world bull riding title. In the fifth round, when the rankest bulls there (the TV pen, that also buck in round 10) were out, my bull fell down coming out of the chute. I was only 65 points on him, but because three other guys had ridden their bulls I had fourth in the round sewn up. Because the bull fell I had the option of a reride. When I took that reride, everybody thought I was crazy.

Guys were running up to me saying, "Do you realize you have fourth place won? What are you doing?" But I didn't hesitate with my decision, because I didn't go there to win fourth. I went there to try to win first. I was 80 points on my reride bull, and moved up to second in the round, which as it turned out was the difference between being the world champion and the runner-up.

I didn't know it would make the difference in the world title when I made the decision, but I will never lay down and settle for fourth if I have a chance to do better. If I'd bucked off that reride bull I would have been the runner-up. But 10 times worse than taking that reride and getting bucked off would have been not taking that reride and losing by $95. If I'd had that chance to make my own outcome and done nothing about it I would have had a hard time living with that because it goes against everything I believe in.

I think the reason that first world bull riding championship meant so much to me was because I was a bull rider before I was anything else. Since I started riding calves when I was 2, I'd already considered myself a bull rider for 10 years before I even started riding in the other roughstock events. Bull riding was the first thing in my life I ever really cared about. As a kid it made me madder to mess up in that event than any of the others. Maybe that explains why my all-around saddles are all displayed on one big rack in my house, and why my bull riding saddles each have their own rack in my living room.

Prizes are cool. I've won trucks, vans, trailers, saddles, buckles, bronzes, watches, silver platters, rings, luggage, rifles, spurs and paintings, and I can point to every prize and tell you a story behind it. Maybe I had to get on three rerides to win it, a late flight almost caused me to miss the rodeo, or I won it after trading the best one away, but the guy I traded with got bucked off. When I'm rocking in a chair with my grandkids, all those memories will be worth more than anything else. I treasure all the prizes, because long after my rodeo days are over, the prizes will remind me of these times and all the funny, happy, sad, scary things that have happened to me in my career.

I won $80,613 at the 1994 NFR and $246,170 for the year. My sixth world all-around championship tied Tom Ferguson and Larry Mahan's record for the most all-around titles ever, which was a great compliment to me. I was on top of the world. I was genuinely happy. My career was going great, and I thought my life was perfect. Surely, I

153

was the luckiest guy in the world. But I know as well as anyone that there are no guarantees in rodeo. That's just part of the deal. Six months later, my knee popped in the middle of that bull ride in Rancho Murieta, and I was forced to take an unexpected year off.

I was in the lead in the world all-around standings and on track to make history with a seventh world all-around title at the time. But it wasn't in the cards. Instead of going on to Reno with the rest of that year's contenders I headed for the operating room. Suddenly, my future was one big fat question mark. Doubters said I was done. Some of my sponsors even walked. Talk about life being lonely at the top. I knew then that the rest of the story was up to me.

December 13, 1998 was, without a doubt, the greatest day of my life. The fact that it fell on my mom's 55th birthday was a bonus, but that's the day, during the 10th round of the 1998 National Finals Rodeo, that I realized my lifelong dream. It's hard to explain in words, but when the whistle blew on my last bull it was like time stopped. I've never had a more clear moment in my life. The whole world stood still in my mind and everything I'd been through since I was a little boy — the fun, the triumphs, the tears and the tragedies — flashed before my eyes. I've never felt happier than at that split second.

The road that led me to that moment was such a mixed bag. After winning six straight all-around championships and rolling along all those years without any serious setbacks, injuries threw a roadblock in my path to the seventh one. What had felt pretty easy got hard real fast, and the disappointments never seemed to end. First the surgeries on both of my knees. Then operations on both shoulders. I kept fighting my way back through all the frustrations, but I finally quit telling people how good I felt each time I came back because I didn't know what was around the next corner.

Every time an injury punched me in the gut I felt a little more determined to overcome it. I was hurt. And when you're hurt you're hurt. I could have cried and whined about it, but I knew that wasn't going to fix my shoulders or my knees. I had two choices: to get up and go on or give up. That second choice wasn't an option for me, and I knew that without having to stop and think about it.

Plan A included countless hours at the gym and a lot of sweat. My gym in Stephenville is an old meat locker. It's not exactly luxurious, and there's no heating or air conditioning. So in the winter it's a chilly 30 degrees in there, and by summer it hits a sweltering 110. But I figured tough conditions would make me tougher, so I took a pass on the fancy gym across town. In the summertime, I was soaked through my shirt before I even started my workout. That just gave me another chance to ask myself how bad I wanted it. I can honestly say that, "More than anything else in the world" was my answer every time.

Whenever you work half that hard for something you really want it means a lot. The seventh all-around championship's a little different than the others in that it wasn't expected of me. So many people, whether they'll admit it now or not, gave up on me when I was hurt so long. They thought I was done. But my family and closest friends knew better than to give up on me. They knew how hard I was working to get back, and never quit believing in me. So when I won the seventh championship those were the people I celebrated with.

There were so many behind-the-scenes type people who helped make my dream come true. Besides my family and all my buddies, I owe a lot to Cody Lambert and Chad Klein. Cody's the master at the entering game, and he entered me all year just because he's my friend. It helped me a ton, and there was nothing in it for him. That's a true friend. I traveled with Chad all year in 1998, and thanks to him I finally understood what I'd done for Cody when we started traveling together 10 years earlier, back when I was the rookie and he was the veteran. Chad's young and enthusiastic, and he can't wait to get to the next rodeo. Ten years into my professional career, that attitude helped pump new life back into me. Genuine enthusiasm is contagious, and a strong dose of it from Chad did me a lot of good.

The first hand I shook when I walked out the gate after my last bull at NFR '98 was Larry Mahan's. I hadn't even had time to take my riding glove off. That meant a lot to me. Not only did he, timed-event great Tom Ferguson and I share the six-championship record all those years, but Larry's always been a special person in my life. He's been my hero and my friend.

I've set other records in my career, and I appreciate them all. But I didn't realize they were records until I had them; they were never goals of mine. The record seventh world all-around championship was more than a goal to me — it was everything. Every professional sport keeps all kinds of stats on all kinds of records, and most of them are broken on a pretty regular basis.

Take baseball, for example. There are records for everything from most runs batted in in one game to most strikeouts and double plays in a game. Then there are those rare records that really mean something. When they're broken, it's a big deal and something everybody talks about for a long time. Mark McGwire did that in baseball (with the home run record) in 1998. I did it in rodeo in 1998. I've had a lot of great times in my career, but in my mind they all pale next to the seventh all-around championship.

I entered the PBR events and whatever rodeos fit into that schedule in 1999. After a record Fourth of July run that was worth almost $42,000, it looked like I was headed back to the NFR in all three events. Then I hyperextended my riding-arm elbow, and had to take some more time off. I went ahead and qualified for the NFR in the saddle bronc riding anyway, and had a $17,385 week there. I won $138,963 in the PRCA in 1999, which wasn't bad for as few rodeos as I got to go to.

But my biggest accomplishment of the year was winning the 1999 PBR Bud Light Cup World Championships. I placed in all five rounds, and won a record $265,912 at the four-day Finals and a record $395,725 for the PBR season. When it was all said and done, I had a $534,688 year. That was something no cowboy had ever done before, and it was pretty cool considering I got to spend so much time at home on the ranch.

I stepped back right after the 1998 season and realized that I'd gotten everything I could ever want in rodeo. Really, everything I've won from there on is a bonus. Everyone's been asking me, "Why don't you retire? You don't have anything left to prove." But the way I look at it, your rodeo career is a very small part of your life — maybe 10 or 15 out of 80 years. And you only get one window to do it in. It isn't like skipping college and going back later to finish. If you don't take your shot it's gone forever. I feel like the luckiest guy in the world because I've gotten to make a living doing what I wanted to do and I've achieved what I set out to do. But that doesn't change the fact that rodeo's still what I love more than anything.

There were a lot of chances for me to get out of rodeo along the way. All the injuries were my ticket to walk. But I wanted it. I wanted that seventh all-around championship so badly that I stuck with it in all three events, and paid whatever dues I had to pay, to make it work.

This isn't something I want to do until I'm 50 — or even 40. I know I'll miss rodeo when my competitive days are over. For one thing I won't get to see all my best friends all the time, like I do now. That'll be hard. And I'll miss riding, because I love to ride so much. But I don't want to be an old piece of worn-out rawhide. When my rodeo career's over there will still be a lot of life left to live and enjoy. And there are other ways to be involved in the sport. I'm sure I'll never leave rodeo completely.

When the time comes to walk away from rodeo as far as competing goes, I think it'll be surprisingly easy for me

to do because I have no regrets. I'm satisfied with my career, and I feel like the success I've had will make it easier to quit. I've already done everything I set out to do and more; I'm content. I've tried my hardest every step of the way and that's as good as it gets. I've also taken care of business, so I won't wake up one morning when I'm 35 wondering where the glory days went and how I'm going to survive. Some guys don't quit rodeoing because they don't know what else to do; it's all they know. I will go out on top. That's a promise I made myself a long time ago.

Three-time World Saddle Bronc Riding Champ Clint Johnson and Lewis Field are classic examples of guys who did just that. They did what they wanted to do in the arena, and then they moved on — when they still had who knows how many world championships left in them. I respect those guys so much for not sticking around long enough to go downhill, and for working hard to succeed at other ventures after rodeo. Their lives didn't end when they left the arena. Mine won't, either.

I have loved the rodeo life — everything about it — since the day I was born. I've loved going to Calgary, Cheyenne and Salinas with my friends, and not having to work at a 9-to-5 job that bored me. Every day at my office is different, and the craving to make great rides on great animals never goes away. I can honestly say that a day hasn't passed that I didn't think about rodeo. It's on my mind every single day, and has been for as long as I can remember. I don't intentionally think about it or make myself do it — it just happens.

But my ultimate goal has never been to be a good roughstock rider. It's always been to be a great cowboy, a tough cowboy and a good horseman. It was a real honor to be inducted into the ProRodeo Hall of Fame in the summer of 2000. But I don't care about going down in history as a great bull rider, or a great bronc rider. I just hope that when people think back long after my career's over and my name's brought up they'll remember me as a great cowboy.

157

< *Celebrating my 1999 PBR Finals championship after riding Terry Williams' Panhandle Slim for 94 points. I won a record $265,912 at the PBR Finals and a record $534,685 for the year, including PRCA earnings. (Watson Rodeo Photos)*